I ♥ MY BARBECUE

I  MY BARBECUE

MORE THAN 100 OF THE MOST
DELICIOUS AND HEALTHY RECIPES
FOR THE GRILL

HILAIRE WALDEN

NOURISH
EAT WELL, LIVE WELL

First published in the UK and USA in 2017 by
Nourish, an imprint of Watkins Media Limited
19 Cecil Court
London WC2N 4EZ

enquiries@nourishbooks.com

Recipes taken from *The Big Book of Barbecuing &
Grilling*, first published by Duncan Baird Publishing
in 2006

Managing Editor: Rebecca Woods
Designer: Clare Thorpe
Commissioned photography: William Lingwood
Food Stylists: Sunil Vijayakar and Joss Herd
Prop Stylist: Tessa Evelegh and Helen Trent

A CIP record for this book is available from the
British Library

ISBN: 978-1-84899-319-8

10 9 8 7 6 5 4 3 2 1

Typeset in Futura

Colour reproduction by Scanhouse, Malaysia
Printed in China

Publisher's note
While every care has been taken in compiling the
recipes for this book, Watkins Media Limited, or any
other persons who have been involved in working
on this publication, cannot accept responsibility for
any errors or omissions, inadvertent or not, that may
be found in the recipes or text, nor for any problems
that may arise as a result of preparing one of these
recipes. If you are pregnant or breastfeeding or
have any special dietary requirements or medical
conditions, it is advisable to consult a medical
professional before following any of the recipes
contained in this book.

Notes on the recipes
Unless otherwise stated:
Use medium fruit and vegetables
Use medium (US large) organic or free-range eggs
Use fresh herbs, spices and chillies
Use granulated sugar (Americans can use ordinary
    granulated sugar when caster sugar is specified)
Do not mix metric, imperial and US cup measurements:
    1 tsp = 5ml 1 tbsp = 15ml 1 cup = 240ml
The symbols refer to the recipes only, not including
optional ingredients or serving suggestions. Check on
the packaging that all ingredients are dairy-, wheat-
or nut-free, or vegan, as brands can vary.

Symbol key
◌ Dairy-free
◉ Nut-free (coconut is being treated as a nut in this
    book, so recipes with coconut milk have not been
    labelled as nut-free)
◉ Wheat-free
Ⓥ Vegetarian (no meat, game or seafood, but can
    contain dairy and egg products)
◉ Vegan (no meat, game, seafood, dairy or egg
    products)

nourishbooks.com

CONTENTS

INTRODUCTION

The first sign of hot weather makes everyone long to cook over an open fire, so out comes the barbecue. There is no need, though, to restrict your barbecue to summertime use. It can also work well on sunny, still days or in a sheltered spot in spring or autumn, and the recipes in this book will provide you with such a selection of recipes to try that you'll want to barbecue as much as possible.

It is so much easier now that the available equipment has improved in both quality and range. There is a wider choice of fuels, and there are many accessories which make barbecueing easier and extend the types of dish that can be cooked, from simple, fine-mesh grilling baskets that prevent small pieces of food falling onto the fire, to motorized rotisseries for spit-roasts.

Another factor in barbecueing's favour is that it is not an exact branch of cooking. First, the choice and proportions of ingredients in a recipe can be changed to suit your taste, budget or available ingredients. The same applies to flavourings such as herbs and spices. Second, the cooking times can vary due to a number of factors. What you must

do, though, is ensure that meat and poultry are adequately cooked, which is why the optimum temperatures have been quoted on pages 13–15.

It is extremely easy to cook all your barbecued food the way you like it when (as with most things in life) you know how. For example, simply adjusting the height of the grill rack and/or moving the food about on the grill rack can produce far better results. There are many more useful tips for trouble-free, successful barbecues in this book.

Here you will find recipes to suit every occasion, taste and diet. There are simple, traditional dishes, such as Smoky Chicken Wings (see page 36), innovative dishes such as Salmon with Spiced Tea Marinade (see page 101) and dishes taken from world cuisines such as Moroccan Chicken with Tabouleh (see page 32). Bacon-wrapped Sausages (see page 56) will be a hit with children and both vegetarians and vegans will find plenty to satisfy them. If you want to make a special meal using your barbecue, you'll find recipes using ingredients such as scallops, king prawns, lobster or guinea fowl.

HOW TO COOK ON A BARBECUE

There are two main cooking methods used in barbecueing: direct and indirect. Direct is when the food is placed directly above the heat source and is usually turned so that it cooks evenly. This is suitable for small items that take less than 25 minutes to cook, such as steaks, burgers, chops and vegetables. Indirect is when the foods are covered by the lid of a barbecue, or by aluminium foil, and cook by reflected heat, as in a conventional oven. This method is suitable for large pieces of meat or poultry that require long cooking.

COOKING HEATS

Cooking can be done over a high, medium or low heat depending on the type of food.

- The fire is described as hot when the flames have given way to glowing red coals covered with a fine layer of white ash. You should be able to hold your hand 15cm/6in above it for 2 seconds. This heat is used for cooking thin pieces of food such as fish fillets and chipolata sausages.
- When the coals are covered by a thicker layer of white ash, the fire has reached the medium heat used for most of the cooking. You should be able to hold your hand over it for 4–5 seconds.
- If you can hold your hand over the fire for longer than 5 seconds, it is too cool for cooking, but can be used for keeping cooked food warm.

TYPES OF BARBECUE

There is such a wide range of types and styles available that it is worth spending a few moments identifying your requirements: how often you will use the barbecue; where you will be barbecueing; the number of people you are likely to cook for most often; how sophisticated you want the equipment to be; and how much money you want to spend on equipment.

When it comes to deciding on a barbecue, the main points to consider are the sturdiness of the construction not only of the main part of the barbecue but also any shelves, the spacing of the bars on the grill rack, whether the grill rack has a non-stick coating, the position of any air vents, ease of carrying, if it is portable, and how easy it will be to store.

Gas barbecues: these are easy to use and heat up within about 10 minutes. They can be regulated, giving good control of the cooking, and do not produce ash. However, they don't burn at as high a temperature as charcoal or wood and do not generally give the food the same 'barbecued' taste, although ceramic beads and chippings which can be used on the barbecue, and modifications such as 'flavouriser' bars, can create the authentic aroma and taste. Portable gas barbecues are also available but the grill height is usually static.

Hibachi: these cast-iron, trough-like barbecues are heavy but portable. They have short legs and can be used on the ground or on a heat-resistant surface at a comfortable working height. The distance of the cooking rack from the fire is adjustable.

Disposable barbecues: convenient, easy to use and cheap, these barbecues consist of an aluminium foil tray filled with charcoal and a firelighter, covered with a grill. Their limitations are their size, the fact that you cannot adjust the height of the cooking rack or move the food to a cooler part of the grill rack for slightly slower cooking, and a burning time of only about 1 hour.

Braziers: these open barbecues vary in size and can have rotisseries for spit-roasting (powered by electricity, battery or hand), wind shields and hoods. They are usually free-standing with wheels or detachable legs, but make sure the legs are long enough otherwise barbecueing can become back-breaking. They should have several air vents, and the height of the grill rack should be adjustable. Braziers are ideal for single servings of food such as chicken portions, chops, steaks and vegetables.

Pedestal barbecues: also known as pillar barbecues, these have a fire bed in an open-topped 'chimney' which is filled with newspaper. Simply light the paper with a taper and it quickly ignites the fuel in the fire bed. Cooking temperature is reached in 20–25 minutes.

Barrel barbecues: made from cast-iron, these resemble pot-bellied stoves. They are very stable and are used at table height. They have adjustable grill racks and often a stand for a rotisserie, are easy to light (with newspaper or kindling), and can be ready to cook in just 10–15 minutes.

Kettle barbecues: these reliable barbecues come in a range of sizes, from table-top models to free-standing versions up to 60cm/24in in diameter. They have a domed metal lid that reflects the heat onto the food, cooking it quickly and evenly and allowing large pieces of meat or whole chickens to be cooked by indirect heat. The cover excludes air, thus reducing flare-ups. Smoke is contained within the barbecue, which heightens the flavour of the food. The cover can be left open for conventional barbecueing by direct heat.

Hooded barbecues: these are sophisticated, usually large, rectangular barbecues set on a moveable trolley, and with a hinged lid. They come with a temperature gauge, dampers to regulate the airflow, moveable grates and cooking grills. Rotisseries, warming racks and side shelves are also available. They work in the same way as a kettle barbecue.

Permanent barbecues: choose a sheltered site with easy access to the kitchen but not too near the house. Ordinary house-bricks can be used in the construction, but it is a good idea to line them with firebricks as they withstand the heat better. You will also need a metal container to hold the fuel, and a grill or grid, preferably with provision for adjusting its height, such as pegs, nails or bricks projecting from the walls. Or simply buy a pack containing everything you need from a DIY store.

FUELS

Wood: hardwoods such as oak, ash, cherry and apple give off a pleasant aroma and burn more slowly than softwoods. They can also produce sparks and smoke. Wood fires take longer to light than charcoal and need care to keep them burning steadily.

Charcoal: there are two main types for barbecueing:

Lumpwood charcoal: this is hard wood that has been fired in a kiln without igniting the wood but driving out all the by-products, resulting in a very light, black, combustible form of carbon. Good-quality lumpwood charcoal normally comes in larger pieces, making barbecueing easier. Instant-lighting lumpwood charcoal is impregnated with a lighting agent. It comes in bags of about 1kg/2lb 4oz; you simply put one of these in the hearth and light it with a match. Once it is alight, more fuel can be added to the hearth if and when necessary to give a bigger fire.

Charcoal briquettes: these uniformly shaped lumps of fuel are made from particles of waste charcoal combined with a starch binder. Once lit, they tend to burn for longer than lumpwood charcoal. (There are also other cheaper briquettes available which are made from alternative sources of fuel, packed out with products such as sand, sawdust and anthracite and bound with a petroleum-based substance. Needless to say, they do not burn as well or for as long as charcoal briquettes. Recycled briquettes made from wood prunings are also available.)

Heat beads: these generate high temperatures for long periods and can be used on open charcoal and kettle barbecues.

Aromatic additives: woodchips impregnated with mesquite or hickory can be scattered over hot charcoal to give a pleasant wood-smoke aroma and flavour. They can be used dry, but if soaked for 1–2 hours before use they will last longer. You can also use woody herbs (such as rosemary, thyme, sage, bay or juniper) and dried fennel stalks on the coals.

BARBECUEING EQUIPMENT

Equipment can divided into a few essentials which you will need to get you started, and extra items you can buy as the barbecueing bug takes hold.

ESSENTIAL

Long-handled tongs, large spatulas and long-pronged fork: use the fork only towards the end of cooking to test if the food is done. If the food is pierced while it is cooking, it will allow juices to escape and the food will become dry.

Long-handled basting brush: choose a natural bristle one.

Skewers: choose long, flat metal ones for meat, poultry and firm-textured fish kebabs, and for keeping spatchcocked birds and butterflied joints flat during cooking. Metal skewers should be oiled before use to prevent food sticking to them. Long and short bamboo and wooden skewers are best for quicker-cooking, smaller and more delicate items; they should be soaked in water for 30 minutes before use to prevent them burning. Wooden cocktail sticks/toothpicks will secure stuffed foods and hold rolled items in place.

Oven gauntlets or oven gloves

Long matches, if using a charcoal fire

USEFUL BUT NOT ESSENTIAL

Hinged baskets: these are useful for cooking a whole large fish or several small fish, or foods such as sausages, burgers and kebabs. They facilitate the turning of foods and help prevent large or more delicate items breaking up.

Fine, wire-mesh racks: these rest on the bars of the grill rack, and are ideal for cooking smaller items that might otherwise break up or fall through the bars.

Wire brush and scraper: for cleaning the grill rack.

Meat thermometer: for testing the internal temperature of large cuts of meat.

Heavy-duty foil drip tray: place under the food to catch any drips and thus prevent flare-ups.

Kebab rack

Barbecue griddle or frying pan (with holes in the base)

SITING AND LIGHTING

Here are a few essential guidelines to help you get the best from your barbecue.
- Always read the manufacturer's instructions for the barbecue and the fuel.

- Choose a place away from overhanging trees or bushes, set free-standing models up where they won't wobble and place portable barbecues on the ground or on a heatproof surface.
- Do not light a fire in high winds or where there is a strong draught.
- Start building a charcoal fire 45–60 minutes before you want to start cooking (30–35 minutes for instant-lighting coal briquettes). Open all the air vents or dampers. Arrange a heap of smaller pieces of fuel in the base of the fire basket. Make a well in the middle and put a solid fire lighter in the bottom. Light the firelighter with a taper and, using larger pieces of fuel, build an igloo-shaped dome on top, enclosing the fire but leaving an airspace. Leave it undisturbed for 30–40 minutes. Once the flames have subsided and the coals are covered with fine white ash, rake them evenly over the base of the barbecue. The fire is ready.
- 'Chimneys' can be bought (or improvized from a large, thoroughly cleaned metal can) to hasten the initial heating. The fuel is packed inside, lit, then, when ready, the coals are tipped in an even layer into the base of the barbecue.
- To top up the fire, first place extra fuel around the outside to warm up, then move a few pieces at a time into the fire.

FOOD SAFETY

There are a few rules to which you should always adhere.
- Don't leave raw or pre-cooked food lying in the sun.
- Keep cooked food well away from raw food, and use separate equipment for preparing and handling each type.
- Always allow frozen food to thaw completely before cooking.
- Keep food cool before cooking; make use of cool boxes.
- Meat is a poor conductor of heat, so thick pieces will take a surprisingly long time to cook. Meat and poultry are cooked when the juices run clear.
- Use a meat thermometer to check the internal temperature of large pieces of meat to ensure the meat is cooked through.

COOKING SAFETY

To ensure your barbecues are safe and fun, follow these guidelines.
- Never use petrol, paraffin or white spirit on a charcoal fire. When it ignites, the fire can run back to the can and cause an explosion.
- Check the hose and regulator on a gas barbecue.
- Keep matches away from a lit fire.
- Have a water spray or bottle of water handy to douse any small flames.

- If there are more serious flames, smother them with a heat-proof lid or other cover.
- Lift a barbecue cover carefully and away from you, to avoid being burned by the steam and blinded by the smoke.
- Do not wear flowing or very loose clothes (be especially careful with sleeves).
- Wear long barbecue gloves and use long-handled barbecue tools, such as tongs and spatulas, for turning and moving foods (use separate tools for moving coals), and a basting brush.
- Never leave a barbecue unattended, and keep children and pets away from the fire.
- When the cooking is complete, push the coals away from the middle to speed the cooling. Charcoal takes a long time to go out; embers that look grey may still be hot.
- Do not move or pack up a charcoal barbecue until the fire is out and the coals are cold.
- Clean the grill rack well with a stiff wire brush and scraper before putting it away.

HINTS AND TIPS

Before starting to cook always:
- Make sure you have enough fuel for the amount of food you want to cook.
- Have everything you will need.
- Heat the fire in plenty of time according to the fuel being used.
- Position the grill rack about 5cm/2in above the heat.

- Brush the grill rack or basket with oil and put it over the fire to heat for a few minutes.
- Soak wooden skewers in water for 20–30 minutes (use them for foods with shorter cooking times). Oil metal skewers (long, flat ones are best for meat, fish, poultry and kebabs that require longer cooking).
- When making kebabs, use foods that take the same amount of time to cook and cut them to the same size. Do not pack meat and poultry too tightly onto skewers otherwise they will not cook through.
- If food has been left in the refrigerator to marinate, move it to room temperature about 30–45 minutes before cooking.
- Brush surplus marinade from foods before cooking them (to keep food moist, brush with left-over marinade during cooking).

During cooking:
- Don't put too much food on the grill rack at a time as the food will steam and never get a crisp, caramelized, tasty surface.
- Leave the food to cook for at least 1 minute when you first place it on the barbecue. Don't try to turn or move it until it can be moved easily.
- Place longer-cooking food on the grill rack first, then add quicker-cooking items.
- Sear meat, poultry and thicker pieces of fish over the hottest part of the fire, then move them to a cooler part, or raise the grill rack, to finish cooking.

- The heat from the fire crisps the surface of the food quickly, but the food itself cooks more slowly and steadily. Meat, poultry and fish in particular will cook better on a relatively cool fire that is glowing gently, usually referred to as medium-hot.
- If fat, oil or marinade drips onto the hot fire and flare-ups occur, remove the food, then either sprinkle the flames with water or wait until they die down before continuing.
- Cook thicker pieces of food towards the edge of the fire because this allows plenty of time for the heat to penetrate to the middle before the outside becomes tough.
- If food seems to be cooking too quickly, raise the rack, or move the food to the edge of the grill rack. If the food is cooking too slowly, lower the grill rack, or move the food towards the middle.
- To cool a fire that's too hot, push the hot coals apart. Conversely, to increase the heat, heap the coals together.
- Check frequently for doneness. Start checking before the food is due to be ready because once it has become dry and tough it's beyond repair.
- Metal skewers will retain heat for quite a while after being removed from the grill rack, so be sure to warn diners about this.
- Be careful about brushing nearly cooked food with marinade containing raw juices, especially a marinade which has been used for chicken or pork.

COOKING TIMES

These cooking times and those given in the recipes are only a guide. The time depends on: the thickness of the food; the temperature of the food and the surroundings; the type of barbecue used; the choice of fuel; the intensity of the heat; the height of the grill rack from the heat source; and whether there are any draughts.

Joints of meat can be tested to see if they are done to your satisfaction by inserting a meat thermometer into the thickest part of the meat. Meat to be sliced for serving should be removed from the grill rack to a ridged meat plate or a board, covered with kitchen foil and left to rest for 5–10 minutes before being carved or cut up.

These timings and those given in the recipes are for foods that are at room temperature before being cooked, then cooked over medium-hot coals using the direct method (see page 7), unless otherwise stated.

POULTRY

For chicken and duck breasts with the skin on, cook the skin side first until it is crisp, then turn them over to complete the cooking. To check if chicken is cooked through, pierce the thickest part, next to the bone if appropriate, with a skewer or the point of a sharp knife. If the juices run clear, the chicken is ready. If the juices are at all pink, it needs more cooking.

The internal temperature should read 82°C/180°F on a meat thermometer.

Breasts on the bone: 275–300g/10–11oz: 25 minutes, turning regularly

Boneless breasts with skin: 7 minutes on skin side, 5 minutes on the other side

Drumsticks/thighs with bone: 225g/8oz: 15–20 minutes, turning regularly

Boneless thigh: 175g/6oz: 4–5 minutes each side

Large wings: 15–20 minutes, turning regularly

Kebabs: 5 minutes each side

Quarters: 250g/9oz: 25–30 minutes, turning regularly

Halves: 700g/1½lb: 35–40 minutes, turning regularly

Poussins, spatchcocked: 25 minutes

Whole chicken: 1.5kg/3lb cooked over indirect heat: 15 minutes per 450g/1lb plus 15 minutes

Duck breasts: 5 minutes skin-side down, then 8–10 minutes on the other side

PORK

These timings produce pork that is well done but still juicy. The internal temperature should be 75°C/170°F.

Boneless steaks: 2–2.5cm/¾–1in thick: 7–8 minutes each side

Chump or loin chops: 2.5cm/1in thick: 8–10 minutes each side

Kebabs: 12–15 minutes, turning once

Fillets/tenderloin: 450g/1lb: 25 minutes, turning once

Larger joints: cooked over indirect heat: 25–30 minutes per 450g/1lb plus 25 minutes or to the required temperature

BEEF

Rump/sirloin steaks: 2.5–4cm/1–1½in: rare: 3–4 minutes each side; medium: 5–6 minutes each side; well-done: 7 minutes each side

Fillet steaks: 4–5cm/1½–2in: rare: 3 minutes each side; medium: 4 minutes each side; well-done: 6 minutes each side

Kebabs: 8–10 minutes, turning regularly

Joints: cooked over indirect heat: 18–20 minutes per 450g/1lb plus 1 hour

Burgers: 2.5cm/1in thick: rare: 3 minutes each side; medium: 4 minutes each side; well-done: 5 minutes each side

LAMB

These timings are for medium-rare lamb. Decrease the timings slightly for really pink and increase slightly for well done.

Loin chops with bone: 2.5cm/1in thick: 6–7 minutes each side

Boneless loin chops: 3 minutes each side

Fillets: 175g/6oz: 4–5 minutes each side

Leg steaks: 4cm/1½in thick: 5–7 minutes each side

Kebabs: 8–10 minutes, turning regularly

Joints: cooked over indirect heat: 20 minutes per 450g/1lb

FISH AND SHELLFISH

As a general rule, allow 8–10 minutes for each 2.5cm/1in thickness (and half the time for half the thickness). Fish is generally considered to be cooked when the flesh in the middle is just changing from translucent to opaque, although there are some exceptions: salmon is often served less well done, while tuna may be fairly rare.

Steaks: 200–225g/7–8oz, 2.5cm/1in thick: 4–5 minutes each side

Fillets: 3–4 minutes each side, depending on thickness

Kebabs: 3–4 minutes each side

Whole fish: 300–325g/10–11oz: 6–7 minutes each side; 1.5kg/3lb: 12–15 minutes each side

Large raw prawns/shrimp: 2–3 minutes each side

Scallops, shucked: 2–3 minutes each side

Symbol key

🌼 Dairy-free

🥜 Nut-free (pine nuts and coconut are being treated as a nut in this book, so recipes with pine nuts, coconut or coconut milk have not been labelled as nut-free)

🌾 Wheat-free

Ⓥ Vegetarian (no meat, game or seafood, but can contain dairy and egg products)

🌱 Vegan (no meat, game, seafood, dairy or egg products)

POULTRY

When selecting poultry, remember that bone and skin add flavour. The skin also protects the flesh from harsh heat and, when cooked to the proper crispness, adds richness. Take care, though, as fat dripping onto hot coals will cause flare-ups, and bone-in chicken can char on the outside before the flesh near the bone is done. However, boneless, skinless pieces can cook too quickly and dry out. Even if you do not want to eat the skin, it is best to leave it on during cooking.

Move poultry from the refrigerator 30 minutes before cooking it. Shallow cuts in chicken breasts, and deeper ones through to the bone of thighs and drumsticks, allow flavourings to penetrate and help even cooking. Brush chicken, especially boneless and skinless pieces, frequently during cooking with the marinade or oil.

Cook bone-in pieces bone-side down until no longer pink in the middle. Pieces with skin should be seared skin-side down for a couple of minutes (except duck, which should be cooked skin-side down for 5 minutes until the skin is crisp), then turned over to continue cooking. All poultry except duck must be well cooked but not dried out. White meat usually takes less time to cook than darker meat such as thighs and drumsticks (see page 14). If you have a lot of chicken to cook, pre-cook bone-in chicken pieces in the oven at 200°C/400°F/Gas 6 for 15 minutes, then finish the cooking immediately on the grill rack, reducing the usual cooking time by about 10 minutes.

CHICKEN WITH LEMON AND MUSTARD

PREPARATION TIME 10 minutes, plus 2 hours
marinating

COOKING TIME 16–20 minutes

SERVES 4

8 chicken pieces on the bone

LEMON AND MUSTARD MARINADE

2 plump garlic cloves

3 tbsp Dijon mustard

5 tbsp olive oil

5 tbsp lemon juice

½ tsp dried thyme

sea salt and freshly ground black pepper

Cut deep slashes in the chicken, then put in
a single layer in a non-metallic bowl.

Peel the garlic and crush it to a paste with a
pinch of salt. Mix with the remaining ingredients.
Spread evenly over the chicken, turn the pieces
over to ensure they are evenly coated, then cover
and leave in a cool place for 2 hours, turning
occasionally.

Cook the chicken pieces, skin-side down first,
on an oiled grill rack for 8–10 minutes on each
side, turning occasionally, until the skin is golden
and the juices run clear when the thickest part is
pierced with a skewer.

CHICKEN WITH ORANGE AND MINT

PREPARATION TIME 15 minutes, plus
1–2 hours marinating

COOKING TIME 12–16 minutes

SERVES 4

1 tbsp olive oil

1 garlic clove, finely chopped

5 tbsp orange juice

2 tbsp lemon juice

2–3 tbsp chopped mint leaves

pinch of caster/granulated sugar

500g/1lb 2oz chicken breasts

sea salt and freshly ground black pepper

mint sprigs, to garnish

Combine the olive oil, garlic, fruit juices, mint,
sugar and plenty of seasoning.

Slash the chicken with the point of a sharp knife,
lay the pieces in a non-metallic dish and pour over
the marinade. Turn the chicken over so the pieces
are evenly coated, then cover and leave in a cool
place for 1–2 hours, turning occasionally.

Lift the chicken from the dish (reserve the remaining
marinade) and cook on an oiled grill rack for
6–8 minutes a side, brushing occasionally with
the marinade. Serve garnished with mint sprigs.

CHICKEN WITH LEMON, MINT AND CHILLI

PREPARATION TIME 10 minutes, plus
  1–2 hours marinating

COOKING TIME 15 minutes

SERVES 2

4 chicken drumsticks

4 tbsp olive oil

handful of mint leaves (about 20)

juice of 1 large or 2 small lemons

2 garlic cloves, chopped

1 red chilli, deseeded and chopped

2 pinches of saffron threads

sea salt and freshly ground black pepper

lemon wedges, to serve

Cut deep slashes in the drumsticks and put them
in a non-metallic dish.

Put the oil, most of the mint and most of the lemon
juice, the garlic, chilli, saffron and black pepper
into a blender and mix to a soft purée. Pour over
the chicken and turn the chicken over so the
pieces are evenly coated. Cover and leave in
a cool place for 1–2 hours.

Lift the chicken from the dish and cook on an oiled
grill rack for 15 minutes, turning every 3 minutes,
until cooked through. Remove from the grill rack
and sprinkle with salt and the remaining lemon
juice and mint. Serve with lemon wedges.

CHICKEN WITH PESTO AND LEMON

PREPARATION TIME 10 minutes, plus 2 hours
  marinating

COOKING TIME 14–16 minutes

SERVES 4

5 tbsp Pesto (see page 154)

juice of 1 small lemon

1½ tbsp extra virgin olive oil

freshly ground black pepper

4 chicken breasts with skin on, about 175g/
  6oz each

basil sprigs, to garnish

Mix the pesto with the lemon juice, extra virgin
olive oil and black pepper.

Place the chicken in a non-metallic dish. Spread
the pesto mixture evenly over the chicken, cover
and leave in a cool place for at least 2 hours.

Cook the chicken on an oiled grill rack for
7–8 minutes on each side. Remove from the
grill, garnish with basil sprigs and serve.

CHICKEN, MANGO AND MINT KEBABS

PREPARATION TIME 10 minutes, plus 1–2 hours marinating

COOKING TIME 10 minutes

SERVES 4

4 skinless, boneless chicken breasts,
cut into bite-size pieces

1 ripe mango

lime wedges and mint sprigs, to serve

LIME AND MINT MARINADE

juice of 2 limes

4 tbsp olive oil

2 tbsp chopped mint leaves

1 tsp soft brown sugar

sea salt and freshly ground black pepper

Put the chicken in a non-metallic bowl.

Mix together the marinade ingredients. Pour over the chicken and stir gently to ensure that it is evenly coated. Cover and leave in a cool place for 1–2 hours.

Meanwhile, peel the mango and cut the flesh into the same-sized pieces as the chicken.

Lift the chicken from the bowl (reserve any remaining marinade) and thread alternately with the mango onto four skewers. Brush with the remaining marinade and cook on an oiled grill for about 10 minutes until golden and cooked through, turning 2–3 times. Serve the kebabs with lime wedges and mint sprigs.

CHICKEN STRIPS WITH BASIL AND LIME

PREPARATION TIME 10 minutes, plus 1–2 hours marinating

COOKING TIME 10 minutes

SERVES 4

450g/1lb skinless chicken breasts

100ml/3½fl oz/generous ⅓ cup extra virgin olive oil

grated zest of 1 large lime

50ml/2fl oz/¼ cup lime juice

2 tbsp shredded basil leaves

salt and freshly ground black pepper

BASIL AND LIME MAYONNAISE

100g/3½oz/scant ½ cup Mayonnaise (see page 154)

2 tbsp finely shredded basil leaves

juice of ½ lime, or to taste

Cut each chicken breast into three lengthways strips and put into a shallow, non-metallic bowl.

Mix the oil with the lime zest and juice, basil leaves and seasoning, using plenty of black pepper. Pour over the chicken, stir to ensure the chicken is well coated, then cover and leave in a cool place for 1–2 hours.

Meanwhile, make the basil and lime mayonnaise by mixing the mayonnaise with most of the basil leaves, and adding lime juice and black pepper to taste. Finish with the remaining basil.

Lift the chicken from the marinade, thread the strips onto skewers, and then cook on an oiled grill rack for about 10 minutes, turning 2–3 times, until golden and cooked through. Serve the skewers accompanied by the mayonnaise.

CHICKEN WITH LIME AND AVOCADO

PREPARATION TIME 15 minutes, plus
    1–2 hours marinating

COOKING TIME 15 minutes

SERVES 4

8 chicken thighs

2 tbsp olive oil

grated zest and juice of 1 lime

2 garlic cloves, crushed

2 tsp ground cumin

pinch of caster/granulated sugar

2 large avocados

3 tbsp chopped coriander/cilantro leaves

sea salt and freshly ground black pepper

coriander/cilantro leaves and lime wedges, to serve

Using the point of a sharp knife, cut three slashes in each thigh. Lay them in a non-metallic dish. Combine the olive oil, lime zest, half the lime juice, the garlic, cumin, sugar and seasoning. Brush evenly over the chicken and into the slashes. Cover and leave in a cool place for 1–2 hours.

Lift the chicken from the dish. Cook on an oiled grill rack for 15 minutes, turning every 3 minutes until cooked through.

Meanwhile, halve, pit, peel and chop the avocados, then mix with the remaining lime juice and chopped coriander/cilantro. Season. Remove the chicken from the grill rack, garnish with coriander/cilantro and serve with the avocado and lime wedges.

INDIAN CHICKEN

PREPARATION TIME 10 minutes, plus
    1–2 hours marinating

COOKING TIME 15 minutes

SERVES 4

8 chicken drumsticks

naan bread, to serve

coriander/cilantro leaves, to garnish

SPICE MIXTURE

1 onion, chopped

4 garlic cloves, crushed

1 tbsp grated fresh root ginger

3 tbsp Thai fish sauce

100ml/3½fl oz/generous ⅓ cup coconut milk

1 tbsp garam masala

1 small handful coriander/cilantro leaves

sea salt and freshly ground black pepper

Cut deep slashes in each chicken drumstick and place in a non-metallic dish.

Make the spice mixture by putting all the ingredients in a blender and pulsing until smooth. Pour over the chicken and turn the pieces so they are evenly coated. Cover and leave in a cool place for 1–2 hours, turning occasionally.

Cook the chicken on an oiled grill rack for 15 minutes, turning every 3 minutes, until cooked through. Meanwhile, warm the naan bread on the side of the grill rack for 30 seconds on each side. Remove the chicken from the grill rack, sprinkle with salt and garnish with coriander/cilantro leaves.

BRONZED CHICKEN THIGHS

PREPARATION TIME 5 minutes

COOKING TIME 15 minutes

SERVES 4

2 tbsp olive oil, plus extra for brushing

1 tsp pimenton (smoked paprika), or sweet paprika

1 tbsp sun-dried tomato purée/paste

juice of ½ lemon

1 garlic clove, crushed

1½ tsp sweet chilli sauce

8 chicken thighs

sea salt and freshly ground black pepper

thyme leaves, to serve

Mix together the olive oil, pimenton, tomato purée/paste, lemon juice, garlic and sweet chilli sauce to form a thick paste.

Brush the thighs with oil and cook on an oiled grill rack for 7 minutes, turning once, then brush generously with the paste and cook for a further 7 minutes or so until the juices run clear when the thickest part is pierced with a skewer.

Remove from the rack, sprinkle with seasoning and thyme leaves, then serve.

THAI-STYLE CHICKEN

PREPARATION TIME 10 minutes, plus 2–3 hours marinating

COOKING TIME 15 minutes

SERVES 6

3 boneless chicken breasts with skin on, about 175g/6oz each

6 chicken drumsticks

lime wedges, to serve

THAI MARINADE

2 shallots, finely chopped

2cm/¾in piece fresh root ginger, grated

1 lemon grass stem, peeled and finely chopped

2 garlic cloves, finely chopped

1 red chilli, deseeded and finely chopped

3 tbsp chopped coriander/cilantro leaves

5 tbsp lime juice

1 tsp caster/granulated sugar

1 tbsp sesame oil

few drops Thai fish sauce, to taste

Cut deep slashes in the chicken pieces and put in a single layer in a shallow, non-metallic dish. Mix all the marinade ingredients, pour over the chicken and turn so they are coated. Cover and leave in a cool place for 2–3 hours, turning occasionally.

Lift the chicken from the dish and cook on an oiled grill rack, allowing 7 minutes on each side for the breasts and 15 minutes for the drumsticks, turning every 3 minutes, until browned and cooked through. Cut the breasts in half and serve with lime wedges.

ITALIAN-STUFFED CHICKEN BREASTS

PREPARATION TIME 15 minutes

COOKING TIME 20 minutes

SERVES 4

40g/1½oz/⅓ cup pine nuts
50g/2oz/3½ tbsp unsalted butter, softened
1 tsp chopped parsley leaves
1 tsp snipped chives
1 tsp chopped tarragon leaves
4 skinless, boneless chicken breasts
12 sun-dried tomatoes, drained
4 large slices of prosciutto
olive oil, for brushing
sea salt and freshly ground black pepper

Toast the pine nuts in a dry heavy-based frying pan, shaking the pan frequently, until lightly and evenly coloured. Reserve 1 tablespoonful. Grind the remaining nuts.

Beat the butter with the herbs and seasoning until smooth and then add the ground pine nuts.

Cut three slits in the top of each chicken breast, going about halfway through the flesh. Tuck a sun-dried tomato in each slit, then press a teaspoonful of the herb butter into each slit and reform the breasts.

Wrap a slice of prosciutto around each chicken breast, overlapping at the ends. Secure with wooden cocktail sticks/toothpicks that have been soaked in water for 10 minutes. Brush with olive oil and season with black pepper.

Cook on an oiled grill rack for 20 minutes, turning once, until the chicken juices run clear when the flesh is pierced with a fine skewer.

BARBECUED CHICKEN DRUMSTICKS

PREPARATION TIME 10 minutes, plus 4–6 hours marinating

COOKING TIME 20–25 minutes

SERVES 4

8 chicken drumsticks

8 baby onions

BARBECUE MARINADE

1 plump garlic clove, finely chopped

120ml/4fl oz/½ cup Home-Made Tomato Ketchup (see page 157)

2 tbsp Worcestershire sauce

1 tbsp Dijon mustard

2 tbsp dark soft brown sugar

Cut a couple of deep slashes in each chicken drumstick and lay them in a large, shallow, non-metallic dish.

Make the marinade by combining the ingredients. Pour evenly over the chicken, then stir the drumsticks around to ensure they are evenly coated. Cover and leave to marinate in a cool place for 4–6 hours, turning occasionally.

Meanwhile, blanch the onions for 5 minutes in boiling water. Drain and dry well. Thread onto skewers.

Lift the drumsticks from the marinade (reserving any remaining marinade). Brush the onions with some of the reserved marinade.

Cook the drumsticks and onions on an oiled grill rack for 15–20 minutes, turning regularly and brushing occasionally with reserved marinade. Serve the drumsticks with the onion kebabs.

TUSCAN CHICKEN WITH TOMATO
AND BLACK OLIVE SALAD

PREPARATION TIME 10 minutes

COOKING TIME 10 minutes

SERVES 4

4–6 garlic cloves

2 tsp salt

1 tsp freshly ground black pepper

3 tbsp finely chopped rosemary leaves

12 skinless, boneless chicken thighs

12 thin slices pancetta

olive oil, for brushing

TOMATO AND BLACK OLIVE SALAD

4 vine-ripened tomatoes, sliced

1 garlic clove, finely chopped

50g/2oz/½ cup oil-cured black olives,
pitted and sliced

3 tbsp extra virgin olive oil

1 tbsp chopped flat-leaf parsley leaves

sea salt and freshly ground black pepper

Make the salad by putting the tomatoes, garlic and olives into a bowl. Season, then trickle over the oil. Scatter over the parsley. Set aside.

Pound the garlic, salt, pepper and rosemary to a paste, using a pestle and mortar, spice grinder or the end of a rolling pin in a small bowl. Rub the paste liberally over the flesh side of the thighs.

Re-shape the thighs and wrap each one in a slice of pancetta. Brush with olive oil. Secure with wooden cocktail sticks/toothpicks that have been soaked in water for 10 minutes.

Cook the chicken thighs on an oiled grill rack for 5 minutes on each side until golden, crisp and cooked through. Remove the thighs from the grill rack. Season with black pepper and serve accompanied by the salad.

TANDOORI CHICKEN KEBABS

PREPARATION TIME 10 minutes, plus 2 hours marinating

COOKING TIME 10 minutes

SERVES 4

8 boneless chicken thighs, cut into approximately 2.5cm/1in pieces

TANDOORI MARINADE
240ml/8fl oz/1 cup yogurt
2 garlic cloves, finely chopped
2 tsp grated fresh root ginger
½ red chilli, deseeded and finely chopped
1 tsp ground cardamom
1 tsp ground coriander
1 tsp garam masala
1 tsp ground cumin
sea salt

Put the chicken in a shallow, non-metallic dish.

Make the marinade by stirring the ingredients together. Pour over the chicken and turn the pieces over to ensure they are coated thoroughly and evenly. Cover and leave in a cool place for 2 hours, turning occasionally.

Drain the chicken from the marinade and thread onto skewers. Cook the chicken on an oiled grill rack for 5 minutes on each side, turning occasionally, until browned and the juices run clear when the thickest part is pierced with a skewer.

MOROCCAN CHICKEN WITH TABOULEH

PREPARATION TIME 15 minutes, plus 2–5 hours marinating

COOKING TIME 10 minutes

SERVES 2

6 boneless chicken thighs, cut into approximately 2.5cm/1in pieces

2 tbsp olive oil

5 tbsp lemon juice

1 plump garlic clove, finely chopped

small handful coriander/cilantro leaves, finely chopped

small handful flat-leaf parsley leaves, finely chopped

1 tbsp ground cumin

1 tbsp cinnamon

1 tbsp ground coriander

salt and freshly ground black pepper

TABOULEH

50g/2oz/⅓ cup bulgur wheat

115g/4oz Italian mixed peppers in oil, drained and chopped

2 tbsp olive oil

2 tbsp lemon juice

handful flat-leaf parsley leaves, finely chopped

4 large sprigs of mint leaves, finely chopped

Thread the chicken onto skewers. Lay the thighs in a single layer in a non-metallic dish.

Combine the olive oil, lemon juice, garlic, herbs, spices and seasoning. Pour over the chicken, turn the thighs over to ensure they are well coated, then cover and leave to marinate in a cool place for 2–5 hours.

Meanwhile, make the tabouleh by putting the bulgur into a bowl. Pour over 60ml/2fl oz/ ¼ cup boiling water over and leave for 30 minutes until the water has been absorbed. Stir occasionally.

Fluff up the bulgur with a fork. Fork through the remaining tabouleh ingredients and season.

Lift the chicken from the dish (reserve the marinade) and cook on an oiled grill rack for 5 minutes on each side, brushing with the reserved marinade occasionally, until cooked through. Using a fork, slip the cooked chicken from the skewers onto the tabouleh.

TURKISH CHICKEN WRAPS

PREPARATION TIME 10 minutes, plus 1–3 hours marinating

COOKING TIME 14–16 minutes

SERVES 4

4 skinless, boneless chicken breasts

2 garlic cloves, peeled

½ tsp ground cinnamon

½ tsp ground allspice

4 tbsp Greek yogurt

3 tbsp lemon juice

1 tbsp olive oil

4 pitta breads

salt and freshly ground black pepper

shredded Iceberg lettuce and sliced tomatoes, to serve

CORIANDER/CILANTRO AÏOLI

3 garlic cloves, chopped

2 egg yolks

juice of 1 lime, or to taste

300ml/10fl oz/1¼ cups groundnut oil

sea salt and freshly ground black pepper

small handful coriander/cilantro leaves, chopped

Put the chicken into a non-metallic dish.

Crush the garlic with a pinch of salt, then mix with the spices, yogurt, lemon juice, oil and black pepper. Coat the chicken evenly with the mixture. Cover and leave to marinate in a cool place for 1–3 hours, turning occasionally.

To make the aïoli, put the garlic, egg yolks and lime juice into a blender and mix briefly. With the motor running, slowly pour in the oil until the mixture becomes thick and creamy. Season and transfer to a bowl. Cover and chill, if liked. Stir in the coriander/cilantro. Serve within 30 minutes.

Lift the chicken from the marinade. Cook on an oiled grill rack for 7–8 minutes on each side, turning once, until cooked through. Remove from the grill rack, cover and leave for 5–10 minutes before slicing.

Meanwhile, warm the pitta breads on the side of the grill rack for 30 seconds per side. Split each one open and stack the two halves on top of each other, cut-side uppermost. Divide the lettuce and tomatoes among the pitta stacks. Lay the chicken on top, then add some aïoli. Roll up the pitta breads around the filling.

ASH-BAKED CHICKEN THIGHS

PREPARATION TIME 10 minutes

COOKING TIME 35 minutes

SERVES 3–6

6 chicken thighs on the bone
4 tbsp finely chopped parsley leaves
5 garlic cloves, thinly sliced
1 lemon, very thinly sliced
sea salt and freshly ground black pepper

Wrap two chicken thighs with one third of the parsley, garlic, lemon and seasoning in a loose parcel of double-thickness, heavy-duty foil. Twist the edges together to seal tightly. Wrap securely in a third piece of foil. Repeat with the remaining chicken to make two more parcels.

Push the hot coals to one side of the fire, add the chicken parcels in a single layer and scatter hot coals in an even layer on the top. Cook for 35 minutes, then carefully remove the parcels and leave to stand for 5–10 minutes before opening. Check that the chicken is cooked through before serving.

SMOKY CHICKEN WINGS

PREPARATION TIME 5 minutes

COOKING TIME 20–25 minutes

SERVES 4

2 tbsp olive oil
1 tbsp sun-dried tomato purée/paste
1 garlic clove, finely crushed
2 tsp sweet chilli sauce
juice of ½ lemon
1 tsp pimenton (smoked paprika)
12 large chicken wings
thyme leaves, for sprinkling
salt and freshly ground black pepper

Combine all the ingredients, except the chicken, thyme and seasoning, to make a thick sauce.

To make it easier to turn the chicken wings on the grill rack, cut off the tips of the chicken wings, then thread three wings onto two parallel skewers. Repeat with the remaining wings.

Cook on an oiled grill rack for 10 minutes, turning twice. Brush liberally with the sauce and cook for a further 10–15 minutes, until cooked through and a rich golden brown, turning and brushing with the sauce occasionally.

Remove from the grill rack, sprinkle with the thyme leaves and seasoning, and serve.

JERK CHICKEN

PREPARATION TIME 10 minutes, plus 2 hours
    marinating

COOKING TIME 20–25 minutes

SERVES 6

6 whole chicken legs

JERK SAUCE

1 onion, coarsely chopped

120ml/4fl oz/½ cup white wine vinegar

120ml/4fl oz/½ cup dark soy sauce

50g/2oz fresh root ginger, coarsely chopped

leaves from small bunch thyme sprigs

1–2 red chillies, deseeded and finely chopped

½ tsp ground allspice

freshly ground black pepper

Put the chicken in a large, shallow, non-metallic
dish.

Make the jerk sauce by combining the ingredients
in a blender until smooth. Pour evenly over the
chicken, turn the pieces over to ensure they are
evenly coated, then cover and leave in a cool
place for 2 hours, turning occasionally.

Lift the chicken from the marinade (reserve any
remaining marinade) and cook, skin-side down
first, on an oiled grill rack for 20–25 minutes,
turning and brushing occasionally with the
reserved marinade, until the skin is golden and the
juices run clear when the thickest part is pierced
with a skewer.

CHICKEN YAKITORI

PREPARATION TIME 10 minutes

COOKING TIME 13–15 minutes

SERVES 6

6 boneless chicken thighs, cut into 2.5 cm/
    1in pieces

12 baby leeks, outer leaves removed, cut into
    2.5 cm/1in lengths, or 12 fat spring onions/
    scallions, green parts trimmed

YAKITORI SAUCE

175ml/6fl oz/¾ cup dark soy sauce

6 tbsp saké

6 tbsp chicken stock

3½ tbsp mirin

1 small garlic clove, finely chopped

1½ tbsp caster/granulated sugar

freshly ground black pepper

Make the sauce by heating the ingredients in a
saucepan, stirring until the sugar has dissolved.
Bring to the boil, then simmer for 1 minute. Remove
from the heat, leave to cool and then strain. Pour
about one quarter of the sauce into a small bowl
to serve as a dipping sauce.

Thread the chicken, skin-side out, and the leeks or
spring onions alternately onto skewers.

Cook the skewers on an oiled grill rack for
2 minutes, brush with the remaining sauce and
continue cooking for 6–8 minutes, basting with
the sauce frequently and turning once. Serve the
skewers with the dipping sauce.

CAJUN CHICKEN WITH TOMATO SALSA

PREPARATION TIME 10 minutes, plus 2–3 hours marinating

COOKING TIME 15 minutes

SERVES 6

2 tsp dried thyme

2 tsp dried oregano

2 tsp paprika

1 tsp ground cumin

1 tsp cayenne pepper

6 boneless chicken breasts, with skin on

groundnut oil, for brushing

sea salt and freshly ground black pepper

lime quarters, to serve

TOMATO SALSA

700g/1½lb firm but ripe plum tomatoes, diced

1 red onion, finely chopped

1 small red chilli, deseeded and finely chopped

1½ tbsp chopped coriander/cilantro leaves

1½ tbsp balsamic vinegar

3 tbsp olive oil

Mix together the herbs, spices and seasoning. Brush the chicken lightly with oil, then rub the spice mixture into the chicken. Cover and leave in a cool place for 2–3 hours.

Meanwhile, make the salsa by combining the ingredients. Add salt to taste. Cover and chill.

Thread the lime quarters onto skewers to grill, if preferred.

Cook the chicken on an oiled grill rack for about 15 minutes until browned and cooked through, turning once. If grilling the limes, cook the skewers alongside until caramelized. Serve the chicken with the lime quarters, either fresh or grilled as above, and accompanied by the salsa.

ORIENTAL CHICKEN WITH FRUITED NOODLE SALAD

PREPARATION TIME 15 minutes, plus 4–6 hours marinating

COOKING TIME 15 minutes

SERVES 4

8 chicken drumsticks

4 tbsp hoisin sauce

2 tbsp clear honey

2 tbsp Home-Made Tomato Ketchup (see page 157)

1 tbsp Chinese five-spice powder

dash of Tabasco sauce

1 garlic clove, peeled

sea salt and freshly ground black pepper

FRUITED NOODLE SALAD

6 tbsp extra virgin olive oil

2 tbsp balsamic vinegar

1 tsp sun-dried tomato purée/paste

225g/8oz fine egg noodles

2 ripe peaches or nectarines, pitted and chopped

4 ripe purple-skinned plums, pitted and sliced

2 tbsp chopped mint leaves

2 tbsp chopped coriander/cilantro leaves

4 tbsp lightly toasted cashew nuts

Slash each drumstick several times with the point of a sharp knife and lay them in a shallow, non-metallic dish.

Combine the hoisin sauce, honey, ketchup, five-spice powder and Tabasco. Crush the garlic to a paste with a pinch of salt and add to the other ingredients, plus some black pepper. Spoon evenly over the chicken, making sure it goes well into the slashes. Cover and leave in a cool place for 4–6 hours, turning occasionally.

Lift the chicken from the dish (reserve any remaining marinade) and cook on an oiled grill rack for 15 minutes until cooked through, turning once and brushing with any remaining marinade.

Meanwhile, make the salad by whisking the oil, vinegar, tomato purée/paste and seasoning together. Cook the noodles according to the packet directions. Drain well and toss them with the dressing. Leave to cool, then mix with the remaining salad ingredients. Serve the chicken with the salad.

TURKEY TIKKA BURGERS

PREPARATION TIME 10 minutes, plus 4 hours
   chilling
COOKING TIME 12–16 minutes
SERVES 4

olive oil, for frying
1 onion, finely chopped
500g/1lb 2oz minced/ground turkey
4 tbsp tikka masala paste
3 tbsp chopped coriander/cilantro leaves
2 tbsp yogurt
1 tbsp mango chutney
sea salt and freshly ground black pepper
4 small naan breads and Raita (see page 156),
   to serve

Heat a little oil in a frying pan, add the onion and
fry until softened. Remove from the heat and leave
to cool.

Mix the onion with the remaining ingredients
until thoroughly combined. With wet hands, form
the mixture into four burgers, 2cm/¾in thick. If
possible, cover and leave in a cool place for 4
hours or overnight to allow the flavours to develop.

Cook the burgers on an oiled grill rack for 6–8
minutes on each side until the juices run clear.

Meanwhile, warm the naan breads on the side
of the grill rack for 20–30 seconds. Serve the
burgers with the raita and naan breads.

TURKEY STEAKS WITH GARLIC, GINGER AND SESAME

PREPARATION TIME 10 minutes, plus
   4–6 hours marinating
COOKING TIME 12 minutes
SERVES 4

4 turkey steaks

SOY AND GINGER MARINADE
3 garlic cloves, finely chopped
2 tbsp grated fresh root ginger
120ml/4fl oz/scant ½ cup dark soy sauce
1 tbsp rice wine or medium sherry
1 tbsp sesame oil
2 tsp sesame seeds
2 tbsp dark brown sugar

Using the point of a sharp knife, make cuts in the
surfaces of the turkey steaks. Lay the steaks in a
single layer in a non-metallic dish.

Combine the marinade ingredients. Pour evenly
over the steaks, then turn them over to coat
thoroughly. Cover and leave in a cool place for
4–6 hours, turning occasionally.

Lift the turkey steaks from the marinade and cook
on an oiled grill rack for about 6 minutes on each
side, turning once, until cooked through.

GUINEA FOWL WITH RUM, ORANGE AND MAPLE SYRUP

PREPARATION TIME 10 minutes, plus 6 hours marinating

COOKING TIME 35 minutes

SERVES 4

1 guinea fowl, about 1.3kg/2½lb, spatchcocked*

2 tbsp dark rum

2 tbsp fresh orange juice, from a bottle or carton

2 tbsp maple syrup

1 tbsp groundnut oil

large pinch of ground allspice

1 tbsp finely chopped fresh root ginger

sea salt and freshly ground black pepper

Thread two oiled metal skewers diagonally through each bird to hold them in shape during cooking. Alternatively, thread one skewer through the wings and body and another skewer through the thighs. Put the guinea fowl into a non-metallic dish.

Combine the remaining ingredients. Brush evenly all over the guinea fowl. Pour any remaining marinade around the bird. Cover and leave in a cool place for 6 hours, basting occasionally.

Lift the bird from the marinade (reserve any remaining marinade) and cook, bone-side down, on an oiled grill rack for 20 minutes. Turn the bird over and cook for a further 15 minutes or so, brushing occasionally with the remaining marinade, until the skin is crisp and the juices run clear when the flesh between the legs and the body is pierced with a skewer.

* If you are unable to buy spatchcocked birds, do it yourself by placing each one in turn on a board. Cut down either side of the backbone with poultry shears or firm, sharp kitchen scissors. Lift out the backbone. Turn the bird over, open it out and press down firmly to open it out flat.

DUCK WITH GINGERED PLUMS

PREPARATION TIME 15 minutes

COOKING TIME 20–25 minutes

SERVES 4

4 Barbary or Gressingham duck breasts

clear honey, for brushing

Chinese five-spice powder, for sprinkling

6 purple-skinned plums, pitted and sliced

1 small garlic clove, finely chopped

4 tsp soy sauce

2 tbsp cider vinegar

2 tbsp sugar

2 tsp grated fresh root ginger

Using a sharp knife, score diagonal parallel lines 1cm/½in apart through the skin of the duck breasts to make a criss-cross pattern; do not pierce the flesh. Brush the breasts with honey, then sprinkle with five-spice powder.

Cook the breasts, skin-side down first, on an oiled grill rack for 5 minutes until the skin is crisp. Then turn the breasts over and cook for a further 8–10 minutes, depending how well done you like your duck to be.

Remove from the grill, cover with foil and leave to rest for 5 minutes.

Meanwhile, put the remaining ingredients into a saucepan, bring to the boil on the side of the grill rack and leave to simmer for 5 minutes.

Sprinkle the duck with seasoning and serve with the plums and juices.

POUSSINS GLAZED WITH HONEY AND SPICES

PREPARATION TIME 10 minutes, plus 4–6 hours marinating

COOKING TIME 25 minutes

SERVES 6

3 large poussins, split down the backbone*

SPICED HONEY MARINADE
2 tbsp sesame oil
2 tbsp white wine vinegar
3 tbsp soy sauce
3 garlic cloves, crushed
2 tbsp clear honey
2.5cm/1in piece fresh root ginger, grated
1½ tbsp finely chopped rosemary leaves
2 tbsp light brown sugar
1 tbsp Dijon mustard
sea salt and freshly ground black pepper

Make the marinade by stirring all the ingredients together until the sugar has dissolved.

Put the poussins in a single layer in a non-metallic dish. Pour over the marinade and turn the birds over to ensure they are evenly coated. Cover and leave to marinate in a cool place for 4–6 hours, turning occasionally.

Drain the marinade from the poussins into a saucepan and bring to the boil on the grill rack.

Cook the poussins, bone-side down, on an oiled grill rack for 15 minutes. Turn them over and cook for a further 10 minutes until the skin is crisp and the juices run clear when the flesh between the legs and the body is pierced with a skewer. Brush occasionally with the marinade.

* If you are unable to buy large poussins, buy medium-sized spatchcocked birds, or spatchcock them yourself by placing each one in turn on a board. Cut down either side of the backbone with poultry shears or firm, sharp kitchen scissors. Lift out the backbone. Turn the bird over, open it out and press down firmly to open it out flat

SPICED GRILLED QUAIL

PREPARATION TIME 15 minutes, plus 1–2 hours marinating

COOKING TIME 15 minutes

SERVES 4–8

8 quails, spatchcocked*
1 tsp fennel seeds, finely crushed
juice of 1½ lemons
3 tbsp extra virgin olive oil
1½ tsp paprika
sea salt and freshly ground black pepper

Thread a skewer through the wings and body of each quail. Thread another skewer through the thighs. Place the quails in a shallow, non-metallic bowl.

Mix the fennel seeds, lemon juice, olive oil, paprika and salt and pepper. Rub thoroughly over the birds, cover and leave in a cool place for 1–2 hours.

Cook the quails on an oiled grill rack, bone-side down, for 8 minutes. Turn them over and cook for a further 5–7 minutes until the skin is crisp and browned and the juices run clear when the thickest part is pierced with a fine skewer.

* If you are unable to buy spatchcocked birds, do it yourself by placing each one in turn on a board. Cut down either side of the backbone with poultry shears or firm, sharp kitchen scissors. Lift out the backbone. Turn the bird over, open it out and press down firmly to open it out flat.

MEAT

When choosing meat for the barbecue, select only lean, tender cuts such as thick sirloin steaks, lamb chops or kebabs made from leg of pork. There is no better treatment for a thick, naturally tender steak than to toss it onto the grill. The high heat delivers a crisp, charred exterior and a juicy interior. The best cuts are sirloin, fillet and T-bone.

Look for steaks at least 2cm/¾in thick, preferably 5cm/2in, as thinner steaks tend to dry out and toughen. Move cuts thicker than 2.5cm/1in to a cooler part of the grill once both sides are well seared so that they continue cooking inside. Add or subtract about 1 minute for every 1cm/½in difference in thickness. Cook over a medium-hot fire, with the grill rack 10–15cm/4–6in above the heat.

Fat dripping onto hot coals can cause flare-ups, so trim any excess (although a little is necessary to give flavour and keep the meat moist) and snip the remainder at 2.5cm/1in intervals to prevent it curling. Fat dripping from sausages can flare up, and there is a risk of undercooking the middle, so you can pre-cook sausages and simply reheat them over the fire. A simple way of testing meat for readiness is to press it lightly with your finger – rare: the meat will give easily and no juices will appear on the surface; medium: the meat will still be slightly springy but a few juices will appear on the surface; well done: the meat will be very firm to the touch and the surface will be covered with juices.

SWEET AND STICKY SPARE RIBS

PREPARATION TIME 5 minutes

COOKING TIME 45–55 minutes

SERVES 4

1.4kg/3lb meaty pork spare ribs

5 garlic cloves, crushed and finely chopped

7.5cm/3in piece fresh root ginger, grated

6 tbsp soy sauce

6 tbsp dry sherry

6 tbsp clear honey

2 tsp chilli sauce

lemon wedges, to serve

Preheat the oven to 190°C/375°F/Gas 5. Lay the ribs in a large foil-lined roasting pan and cook in the oven for about 35–40 minutes until tender.

Combine the garlic, ginger, soy sauce, sherry, honey and chilli sauce to make the baste.

When cooked, brush the ribs liberally and evenly with the baste. Reserve the remaining baste.

Continue cooking the ribs on an oiled grill rack for 10–15 minutes, turning occasionally and brushing with the baste, until the meat is browned and comes off the bone easily. Brush once more and remove from the grill rack.

Transfer to a board and divide into individual ribs. Serve with the lemon wedges.

CHINESE-STYLE RIBS

PREPARATION TIME 10 minutes

COOKING TIME 1 hour

SERVES 4–6

2kg/4lb meaty pork spare ribs

1½ tsp Sichuan peppercorns

150ml/5fl oz/generous ½ cup clear honey

3 garlic cloves, crushed

2 tbsp rice wine or dry sherry

2 tbsp plum sauce

2 tbsp ginger juice (produced by squeezing ginger through a garlic press)

2–3 tsp chilli sauce

1 tbsp Chinese five-spice powder

lime wedges, to serve

Preheat the oven to 190°C/375°F/Gas 5. Lay the ribs in a large foil-lined roasting pan and cook in the oven for about 45 minutes until tender.

Meanwhile, heat a dry, heavy-based frying pan. Add the peppercorns and heat until fragrant. Grind in a spice grinder or in a small bowl using the end of a rolling pin. Combine with the remaining ingredients (except the lime wedges). Brush liberally over the cooked ribs, ensuring they are evenly coated. Reserve the remaining mixture.

Cook the ribs on an oiled grill rack for 10–15 minutes until the meat is browned and comes off the bone easily, turning occasionally and brushing with the remaining mixture. Brush once more and remove from the grill rack. Transfer to a board and divide the ribs. Serve with lime wedges.

PORK BROCHETTES WITH LEMON AND GINGER

PREPARATION TIME 10 minutes, plus 2½ hours marinating

COOKING TIME 12–15 minutes

SERVES 4

550g/1¼lb pork, cut into 3cm/1¼in cubes

juice of 1 lemon

3 garlic cloves, peeled

4 tbsp Greek yogurt

1 tbsp grated fresh root ginger

1 tsp ground cardamom

½ tsp ground cumin

½ tsp grated nutmeg

½ dash Tabasco sauce

1½ lemons

sea salt and freshly ground black pepper

Put the pork into a non-metallic bowl. Stir in the lemon juice and plenty of black pepper. Cover and leave to marinate in a cool place for 30 minutes.

Meanwhile, crush the garlic with a pinch of salt and combine with the yogurt, ginger, cardamom, cumin, nutmeg and Tabasco.

Drain the lemon juice from the pork. Stir in the ginger mixture to coat the cubes evenly and thoroughly. Cover and leave in a cool place for 2 hours.

Meanwhile, cut the lemons into thick slices, then cut the slices in half.

Lift the pork from the ginger mixture, shaking off the excess, and thread onto skewers alternately with the lemon pieces. Cook on an oiled grill rack for 12–15 minutes, turning regularly, until well browned on the outside and cooked through.

SPICED PORK STEAKS

PREPARATION TIME 10 minutes, plus 4 hours
   marinating

COOKING TIME 15 minutes

SERVES 4

4 pork steaks

MARINADE

1 tsp ground cumin

1 tsp dried oregano

½ tsp ground cardamom

½ tsp harissa

½ tsp ground coriander

2 tbsp sun-dried tomato purée/paste

1 tbsp olive oil

4 garlic cloves, crushed

grated zest of 1 lime

3 tbsp lime juice

pinch of caster/granulated sugar

sea salt and freshly ground black pepper

Using the point of a sharp knife, cut three or four
slashes in each pork steak. Place in a shallow,
non-metallic bowl.

Combine all the marinade ingredients and spread
evenly and thoroughly over the pork. Cover and
leave to marinate in a cool place for 4 hours.

Cook on an oiled grill rack over medium-hot coals
for 7–8 minutes on each side, turning once.

PORK AND APPLE SKEWERS

PREPARATION TIME 10 minutes, plus
   3–4 hours marinating

COOKING TIME 12–15 minutes

SERVES 4

450g/1lb pork tenderloin, cut into 3cm/
   1¼in cubes

1 tbsp finely chopped sage leaves

3½ tbsp sharp apple juice

grated zest and juice of ½ lemon

2 tbsp wholegrain mustard

4 tbsp grapeseed oil

2 crisp red apples

a few sprigs of sage

sea salt and freshly ground black pepper

Put the pork into a non-metallic bowl.

Mix the chopped sage leaves with the apple juice,
lemon zest and juice, mustard, oil and salt and
black pepper. Stir into the pork to ensure the cubes
are evenly coated, then cover and leave to marinate
in a cool place for 3–4 hours.

Meanwhile, core the apples and cut into wedges.

Lift the pork from the bowl, reserving the marinade.
Thread the pork and apple alternately onto skewers,
interspersing the pieces with sage leaves.

Cook on an oiled grill rack for 12–15 minutes,
turning regularly and brushing with the remaining
marinade, until the pork is cooked through.

INDONESIAN PORK BURGERS

PREPARATION TIME 10 minutes, plus 10 minutes soaking and 1 hour chilling

COOKING TIME 12 minutes

SERVES 4

3½ tbsp coconut milk
50g/2oz/1 cup fresh breadcrumbs
450g/1lb minced/ground pork
1 garlic clove, finely chopped
2 tbsp Thai red curry paste
2 tbsp chopped basil leaves
1 tbsp chopped coriander/cilantro leaves
1 tbsp Thai fish sauce
grated zest of 1 lime
1 tbsp lime juice
pinch of caster/granulated sugar
groundnut oil, for brushing
sea salt and freshly ground black pepper

Pour the coconut milk over the breadcrumbs and leave to soak for 10 minutes.

Combine the soaked breadcrumbs with the remaining ingredients, mixing thoroughly until well combined. With wet hands, form the mixture into eight equal burgers, 2–2.5cm/¾–1in thick. Chill for an hour or more.

Brush the burgers with groundnut oil and cook on an oiled grill rack, turning once, for about 6 minutes on each side until golden and the juices run clear.

PORK, PANCETTA AND PARMESAN BURGERS

PREPARATION TIME 10 minutes, plus 1 hour chilling

COOKING TIME 12 minutes

SERVES 4

450g/1lb minced/ground pork

75g/3oz pancetta, coarsely chopped

50g/2oz/⅔ cup freshly grated Parmesan cheese

1½ tbsp finely chopped fresh sage

1 egg, beaten

freshly ground black pepper

4 squares of focaccia, halved horizontally

salad leaves, such as rocket/arugula, lamb's lettuce, frisée and radicchio, to serve

Roasted Tomato Salsa (see page 157) or Red Pepper, Black Olive and Caper Relish (see page 159), to serve

Using a fork or your hands, combine the pork, pancetta, Parmesan, sage, egg and black pepper in a large bowl. With damp hands, form into four burgers approximately 2.5cm/1in thick. Leave in a cool place for at least 1 hour.

Cook the burgers on an oiled grill for about 6 minutes on each side, turning once, until the juices run clear.

Meanwhile, warm the focaccia on the side of the grill rack. Top the bottom halves of the focaccia with salad leaves, add the burgers and then a spoonful of the salsa or relish.

HONEY AND MUSTARD GLAZED SAUSAGES

PREPARATION TIME 5 minutes
COOKING TIME 13–15 minutes
SERVES 4

2 tbsp clear honey
2 tbsp wholegrain mustard
juice of 1 small lemon
2 garlic cloves, finely chopped (optional)
8 pork sausages
sea salt and freshly ground black pepper

Mix the honey, mustard, lemon juice and garlic (if using), and season lightly.

Add the sausages to a pan of boiling water, quickly return to the boil and then simmer gently for 3 minutes. Drain and rinse under cold running water to speed cooling. Pat dry.

Brush the sausages with some of the honey mixture, then cook on an oiled grill rack for 8–10 minutes, turning occasionally and brushing with the glaze, until evenly browned and cooked through.

BACON-WRAPPED SAUSAGES WITH MUSTARD DIP

PREPARATION TIME 10 minutes
COOKING TIME 12–14 minutes
SERVES 4–6

12 pork sausages
12 rashers smoked streaky bacon, rinds removed
2 tbsp chopped thyme leaves (optional)

MUSTARD DIP
4 tbsp wholegrain mustard
120ml/4fl oz/½ cup Mayonnaise (see page 154)

Make the mustard dip by beating the mustard into the mayonnaise.

Add the sausages to a pan of boiling water, quickly return to the boil and then simmer gently for 3 minutes. Drain and rinse under cold running water to speed cooling. Pat dry.

Stretch each bacon rasher with the back of a knife. Sprinkle the thyme, if using, over one side of each rasher. Place a sausage diagonally across one end of each rasher and roll up to enclose the sausage completely. Secure with soaked wooden cocktail sticks/toothpicks.

Cook the wrapped sausages on an oiled grill rack for 7–8 minutes until well browned and cooked through, turning regularly.

CHAR SUI PORK

PREPARATION TIME 10 minutes, plus 4–6 hours marinating

COOKING TIME 14–16 minutes

SERVES 4

4 pork shoulder steaks

CHAR SUI MARINADE
1 tbsp sunflower oil
1 tbsp sesame oil
2 tbsp hoisin sauce
2 tbsp clear honey
2 tbsp soy sauce
1 tsp Chinese five-spice powder
freshly ground black pepper
2 garlic cloves, finely chopped
5cm/2in piece fresh root ginger, grated

TO SERVE
6 spring onions/scallions, sliced lengthways into thin shreds
½ cucumber, deseeded and cut into long, thin strips
Chinese plum sauce
lime wedges

Lay the pork steaks in a single layer in a shallow, non-metallic dish.

Make the marinade by stirring together all the ingredients except the ginger. Using a garlic press, squeeze the ginger juice into the other ingredients, then stir in. Pour over the pork, turn the steaks to ensure they are completely coated, then cover and leave to marinate in a cool place for at least 4–6 hours, turning occasionally.

Lift the pork from the marinade (reserve the remaining marinade) and cook for 7–8 minutes on each side, turning once and basting with any remaining marinade, until the juices run clear when the thickest part of the steak is pierced with a skewer. Serve the steaks with the spring onions, cucumber, plum sauce and lime wedges.

GAMMON STEAKS WITH APRICOT GLAZE

PREPARATION TIME 10 minutes

COOKING TIME 10–12 minutes

SERVES 4

4 gammon steaks

APRICOT GLAZE

3 tbsp good-quality apricot jam, warmed slightly

1 tbsp Dijon mustard

2 tsp Worcestershire sauce

freshly ground black pepper

Trim any surplus fat from the steaks, leaving enough to keep them moist. Snip the remaining fat at 2.5cm/1in intervals.

Make the glaze by combining all the ingredients.

Brush the glaze over the gammon steaks and cook on an oiled grill rack for 5–6 minutes on each side, turning once.

SOUVLAKIA

PREPARATION TIME 10 minutes, plus 3–4 hours marinating

COOKING TIME 8–10 minutes

SERVES 6

700g/1½lb lean lamb, cut into 3cm/1¼in cubes

1 large onion

5 tbsp olive oil

4 garlic cloves, coarsely chopped

½ tsp ground cumin

1½ tsp cayenne pepper

sea salt and freshly ground black pepper

pitta breads. lemon wedges and seasoned Greek yogurt with chopped coriander/cilantro leaves stirred in, to serve

Put the lamb into a non-metallic bowl. Put the olive oil, onion, garlic, cumin, cayenne and plenty of black pepper into a food processor or blender and mix until mushy. Tip over the lamb, stir to coat the cubes evenly, then cover and leave in a cool place for 3–4 hours, stirring occasionally.

Lift the lamb from the bowl (reserve the marinade) and thread onto skewers. Cook on an oiled grill rack for 8–10 minutes, turning regularly and brushing with the marinade, until nicely browned on the outside and cooked to your liking inside.

Meanwhile, warm the pitta breads on the side of the grill rack for 30 seconds on each side. Remove the kebabs from the grill rack, sprinkle over some sea salt and a little lemon juice, then serve in pitta breads with a spoonful of the yogurt.

FRAGRANT LAMB KEBABS

PREPARATION TIME 10 minutes, plus
    4–6 hours marinating

COOKING TIME 8–10 minutes

SERVES 6–8

900g/2lb lean lamb, cut into 4cm/1½in cubes

1 lemon, cut into 12 wedges

12 fresh bay leaves

OREGANO MARINADE

4 tbsp olive oil

2½ tsp dried oregano

1 tsp paprika

1 tsp ground cumin

grated rind and juice of ½ large lemon

sea salt and freshly ground black pepper

Put the lamb into a non-metallic dish.

Combine the oil, oregano, paprika, cumin, lemon
rind and juice, and black pepper. Mix with the
lamb so the cubes are evenly coated, then cover
and leave in cool place for 4–6 hours.

Thread the lamb onto skewers alternating with the
lemon wedges and bay leaves. Cook the kebabs
on an oiled grill rack for 8–10 minutes, turning
regularly, until well browned on the outside and
still juicy inside.

LAMB KEBABS WITH SUN-DRIED TOMATOES AND THYME

PREPARATION TIME 10 minutes, plus
    2 hours marinating

COOKING TIME 8–10 minutes

SERVES 4

450g/1lb boneless leg of lamb, cut into
    3cm/1¼in cubes

TOMATO AND THYME MARINADE

150ml/5fl oz/⅔ cup yogurt

3 garlic cloves, finely chopped

4 tbsp red wine

2 tbsp olive oil

2 tbsp sun-dried tomato purée/paste

1 tsp dried thyme

Put the lamb into a non-metallic bowl.

Make the marinade by combining the ingredients.
Stir into the lamb to coat the pieces evenly. Cover
and leave in a cool place for 2 hours.

Lift the lamb from the bowl (reserve any remaining
marinade) and thread onto skewers. Cook on
an oiled grill rack, turning regularly and brushing
with the reserved marinade, for 8–10 minutes until
well browned on the outside and still juicy inside.

LAMB STEAKS WITH ROSEMARY AND LEMON

PREPARATION TIME 5 minutes, plus 3 hours marinating

COOKING TIME 8–12 minutes

SERVES 4

4 lamb leg steaks, 150g/5oz each

juice and zest of 1 lemon

3 tbsp extra virgin olive oil

2 garlic cloves, crushed

leaves from 3 rosemary sprigs, finely chopped

2 lemons, halved

Lay the lamb in a single layer in a shallow, non-metallic dish.

Combine the lemon juice and zest, olive oil, garlic and rosemary. Pour over the lamb, turn the steaks over, cover and leave in a cool place for 3 hours, turning a couple of times.

Lift the lamb from the dish (reserve the marinade) and cook on an oiled grill rack, turning once, for 4 minutes on each side for medium lamb, 6 minutes on each side for well done.

Meanwhile, brush the halved lemons with the remaining marinade and cook, cut-side down, on the grill rack for 4–5 minutes on each side.

KOFTAS

PREPARATION TIME 15 minutes, plus 4 hours marinating

COOKING TIME 10–12 minutes

SERVES 4

1 small onion, quartered

2 garlic cloves, chopped

2.5cm/1in piece fresh root ginger, chopped

1 tsp ground cumin

1 tsp ground coriander

1 tbsp olive oil, plus extra for brushing

450g/1lb minced/ground lamb

3 tbsp chopped coriander/cilantro leaves

1 large egg, beaten

sea salt and freshly ground black pepper

cumin seeds, toasted and crushed, for sprinkling

Raita (see page 156), to serve

lemon wedges, to serve

Put the onion, garlic and ginger in a small blender or food processor and mix until finely chopped. Add the spices and mix again until evenly combined.

Heat the oil in a frying pan, add the onion mix and fry for 2–3 minutes, stirring. Leave to cool.

Put the lamb into a bowl and break it up with a fork. Add the cold onion mix, the coriander/cilantro and seasoning, then mix in enough egg to bind, but don't add so much that the mixture becomes sticky. If time allows, cover and keep in a cool place for up to 4 hours, or overnight in the refrigerator.

Divide the mixture into eight equal portions. With wet hands, mould each portion into a long sausage around a skewer.

Brush the koftas with oil and cook on an oiled grill rack for 8–10 minutes, turning occasionally, until nicely browned on the outside and cooked to your liking inside.

Sprinkle the koftas with the cumin and serve with raita and lemon wedges.

BUTTERFLIED CHINESE LAMB

PREPARATION TIME 15 minutes, plus 8 hours
   marinating

COOKING TIME 30–35 minutes

SERVES 8

1.1kg/2½lb shoulder of lamb

4 garlic cloves, cut into thin slivers

CHINESE MARINADE

150ml/5fl oz/⅔ cup soy sauce

150ml/5fl oz/⅔ cup Madeira or medium
   dry sherry

2.5cm/1in piece fresh root ginger, grated

1 tbsp clear honey

3 star anise

3 tbsp chopped coriander/cilantro leaves

freshly ground black pepper

Make the marinade by mixing all the ingredients
in a blender.

Open out the lamb and cut a few slits all over
the surface. Insert the garlic slivers into the slits.
Put the lamb into a non-metallic dish, pour over
the marinade, cover and leave in a cool place
for 8 hours or overnight, turning occasionally.

Lift the lamb from the marinade (reserving the
marinade) and cook on an oiled grill rack, basting
frequently with the remaining marinade, over a
medium heat for 30–35 minutes for medium rare.

RACK OF LAMB WITH SESAME AND MUSTARD

PREPARATION TIME 10 minutes, plus 2 hours
   marinating

COOKING TIME 15–25 minutes

SERVES 4

2 racks of lamb, 700g/1½lb each, trimmed of
   excess fat

large sprigs of sage, for cooking

GARLIC AND SESAME MARINADE

3 tbsp soy sauce

2 tbsp Dijon mustard

2 tbsp lightly toasted sesame seeds

1½ tbsp sesame oil

1½ tbsp sugar

1 plump garlic clove, finely chopped

1 tbsp sea salt

2 tsp freshly ground black pepper

Make the marinade by stirring all the ingredients
together. Rub over the lamb and leave to marinate
in a cool place for 2 hours.

Just before cooking the lamb, scatter the sage over
the coals. Cover the lamb bones with foil to stop
them burning. Cook on an oiled grill rack, turning
once, for 15 minutes for rare lamb, 20 minutes for
medium rare and 25 minutes for well done.

Remove from the grill rack and leave to rest,
covered, for 10 minutes before dividing into cutlets.

SPICED LAMB CHOPS

PREPARATION TIME 15 minutes, plus 4 hours marinating

COOKING TIME 12–18 minutes

SERVES 4

olive oil, for frying

1 large onion, finely chopped

1 plump garlic clove, finely chopped

1 tbsp coriander seeds, lightly crushed

1 tbsp mustard seeds, lightly crushed

2 tsp cumin seeds, lightly crushed

1 tsp paprika

150ml/5 fl oz/⅔ cup Greek yogurt

sea salt and freshly ground black pepper

8 lamb loin chops

chopped coriander/cilantro leaves

Pineapple and Macadamia Nut Salsa (see page 158), to serve

Heat the oil in a frying pan, add the onion and cook until softened and lightly coloured; stir in the garlic towards the end of cooking. Add all the seeds and cook, stirring, for 1–2 minutes. Transfer the onion mixture to a bowl and stir in the paprika, yogurt and seasoning. Leave to cool.

Coil the 'tail' end of the chops round the eye of the meat and secure with wooden cocktail sticks/toothpicks. Put the chops in a single layer in a shallow, non-metallic dish. Pour over the yogurt mixture, turn the chops over, cover and leave in a cool place for about 4 hours, turning occasionally.

Lift the lamb from the dish. Cook on an oiled grill rack, turning once, for 3 minutes on each side for medium rare or for 5 minutes on each side for well done.

Remove the chops from the grill rack and sprinkle with chopped coriander/cilantro. Serve with the salsa.

BEEF AND MUSHROOM BURGERS WITH ROASTED RED PEPPER DRESSING

PREPARATION TIME 15 minutes, plus 20 minutes soaking and 1 hour chilling

COOKING TIME 13–15 minutes

SERVES 4

2 tbsp dried porcini mushrooms

small knob of unsalted butter

150g/5oz chestnut mushrooms, chopped

1 garlic clove, finely chopped

450g/1lb lean minced/ground beef

4 tsp wholegrain mustard

2 tbsp chopped mixed herbs

sea salt and freshly ground black pepper

4 rolls, split horizontally, and salad leaves, to serve

ROASTED RED PEPPER DRESSING

1 red pepper

2 tbsp balsamic vinegar

1 tsp thyme leaves

1 tsp chopped garlic

6 tbsp olive oil

sea salt and freshly ground black pepper

Place the dried porcini in a bowl and just cover with boiling water. Soak for 20 minutes, then drain, pat dry and chop finely.

Heat the butter in a frying pan, add the chestnut mushrooms and garlic and fry until the liquid has been given off and the mushrooms are tender. Stir in the soaked porcini just before the end of cooking. Leave to cool.

Mix the beef with the mushroom mixture, mustard, herbs (such as marjoram, tarragon, parsley, sage or thyme) and seasoning until thoroughly combined. Divide the mixture into four equal portions. With wet hands, form each portion into a burger approximately 2.5cm/1in thick. If time allows, cover and leave in a cool place for 1 hour, or more, to allow the flavours to develop.

To make the dressing, roast the red pepper whole on an oiled grill rack, or under a preheated grill/broiler, until charred and blistered. Leave until cool enough to handle, then peel off the skin and discard, along with the seeds. Put into a blender with the vinegar, thyme and garlic. Pulse to mix, then, with the motor running, slowly pour in the olive oil until you have a smooth sauce. Season to taste.

Cook the burgers on an oiled grill, turning once, for 4–5 minutes on each side for medium-rare, or for longer if you prefer them more well done.

Meanwhile, toast the rolls on the grill. Mix the salad leaves with a little dressing, then put them on the bottom half of each roll. Top with the burgers and spoon a little more dressing over them. Cover with the top halves of the rolls and serve.

SURPRISE BEEFBURGERS

PREPARATION TIME 10 minutes, plus 2 hours
   chilling
COOKING TIME 10–15 minutes
SERVES 4

1 onion, finely chopped

1 tbsp olive oil

1 plump garlic clove, finely chopped

450g/1lb lean minced/ground beef

2 tsp chopped parsley leaves

sea salt and freshly ground black pepper

50g/2oz feta cheese

4 sesame buns

salad leaves and Home-Made Tomato Ketchup
   (see page 157), to serve

Cook the onion in the oil until softened and lightly
coloured. Stir in the garlic towards the end.
Remove from the heat and leave to cool.

Mix the onion and garlic with the beef, parsley
and seasoning. Divide the mixture into four equal
portions and form into burgers about 10cm/4in
in diameter, enclosing a quarter of the cheese in
each one. Leave in a cool place for 2 hours.

Cook the burgers on an oiled grill rack for
3–4 minutes on each side for medium-rare, or
longer if you prefer the burgers more well done.

Meanwhile, warm the sesame buns on the side of
the rack. Split in half, place salad leaves on the
bottom, top with a burger and ketchup, and close
with the top of the bun.

STEAKS WITH MUSTARD AND SOY

PREPARATION TIME 10 minutes, plus 4 hours
   marinating
COOKING TIME 6–12 minutes
SERVES 4

3 tbsp Dijon mustard

1 tbsp soy sauce

1 tbsp grated fresh root ginger

1 tbsp olive oil

3 tbsp chopped coriander/cilantro leaves

4 rump or sirloin steaks, 2.5cm/1in thick

Mix together the mustard, soy sauce, ginger,
olive oil and coriander/cilantro. Smooth over the
steaks, cover and leave in a cool place for about
4 hours.

Cook the steaks on an oiled grill rack, turning
once, for about 3–4 minutes on each side for
rare steaks, 5–6 minutes on each side for medium
steaks, or until cooked to your liking.

STEAK SANDWICHES WITH ONION RELISH

PREPARATION TIME 10 minutes

COOKING TIME 45–50 minutes

SERVES 4

4 sirloin steaks

olive oil, for brushing

4 small baguettes, about 20cm/8in long

butter, for spreading

Dijon or wholegrain mustard, for spreading

ONION RELISH

2 tbsp olive oil

450g/1lb large onions, sliced thinly into rings

1 tbsp balsamic vinegar

1 tbsp Worcestershire sauce

pinch of brown sugar

sea salt and freshly ground black pepper

Make the onion relish by heating the oil in a large, heavy frying pan. Add the onions and cook very gently, stirring occasionally, until they are soft and tinged with brown. Stir in the vinegar, Worcestershire sauce, sugar and seasoning. Continue to cook until the liquid has evaporated. Check the sweetness and seasoning. Set aside to cool.

Brush the steaks with olive oil and cook on an oiled grill rack for about 3 minutes on each side for rare, 4 minutes for medium, or until cooked to your liking.

Meanwhile, split the baguettes lengthways and warm them on the side of the grill rack. Spread the inside of each bottom half with butter and just a little mustard. Lay a steak in each baguette and top with onion relish. Close the baguettes and eat immediately.

SPICED BEEF KEBABS

PREPARATION TIME 15 minutes, plus 8 hours marinating

COOKING TIME 6–8 minutes

SERVES 4

550g/1¼lb rump steak, cut into
3cm/1¼in cubes

1 red pepper

1 yellow pepper

16 cherry tomatoes

olive oil, for brushing

sea salt and freshly ground black pepper

SPICED MARINADE

8 tbsp Home-Made Tomato Ketchup
(see page 157)

4 tbsp red wine

2 tbsp soy sauce

1 tbsp chilli sauce

2 tsp Jamaican Jerk Seasoning
(see page 159)

Put the beef into a non-metallic bowl.

Make the marinade by combining all the ingredients. Stir into the beef to cover the cubes evenly and thoroughly. Cover and leave in a cool place for 8 hours, stirring occasionally.

Meanwhile, cut the peppers into 2.5cm/1in squares. Stack in pairs of one of each colour. Brush the pepper stacks and the tomatoes with oil and season them.

Lift the beef from the marinade (reserve any remaining marinade) and thread onto skewers, alternating with the pepper stacks and tomatoes.

Cook on an oiled grill rack for 6–8 minutes, turning regularly and brushing with any remaining marinade, until cooked to your liking.

KENTUCKY GRILLED BEEF

PREPARATION TIME 10 minutes, plus 4 hours marinating

COOKING TIME 10–14 minutes

SERVES 6

2 beef fillets, about 350g/12oz each
6 slices sourdough bread, or country bread
Aïoli (see page 156), lettuce and
4–6 tomatoes, to serve

KENTUCKY RUB
1 tbsp paprika
1½ tsp freshly ground black pepper
½ tsp English mustard powder
½ tsp garlic granules
½ tsp dried sage
½ tsp dried oregano
½ tsp ground chillies
sea salt

Using a large, sharp knife held parallel, cut through one side of each fillet going almost but not quite through to the opposite side. Open out flat, like a book.

Make the Kentucky rub by combining all the ingredients. Rub thoroughly into all the surfaces of the beef. Cover and leave in a cool place for about 4 hours.

Reshape each piece of beef and cook on an oiled grill rack for about 5–7 minutes on each side until nicely browned on the outside but still pink in the middle.

Remove the beef from the rack, cover with foil and leave to rest for 5–10 minutes.

Shred a few lettuce leaves and slice the tomatoes. Carve the beef into thin slices and serve with the bread, aïoli, lettuce and tomatoes.

RIB OF BEEF WITH MUSTARD AÏOLI

PREPARATION TIME 10 minutes

COOKING TIME 8 minutes

SERVES 8

1.8kg/4lb rib of beef, cut into individual ribs

sea salt and freshly ground black pepper

MUSTARD AÏOLI

6 plump garlic cloves, crushed

2 egg yolks, at room temperature

juice of 1 small lemon, plus extra, to taste (optional)

425ml/15fl oz/1¾ cups olive oil

3 tbsp wholegrain mustard

Make the mustard aïoli by putting the garlic, egg yolks and lemon juice in a blender and mixing briefly. With the motor running, slowly pour in the olive oil in a thin, steady stream until the mixture becomes the consistency of thick cream. Transfer to a bowl, stir in the mustard and season to taste; add more lemon juice, if necessary.

Meanwhile, lay the ribs on an oiled grill rack and cook for about 4 minutes, turning the ribs through 90 degrees halfway through cooking, to create a criss-cross pattern. Turn them over and repeat on the other side. Cook for longer if you prefer well-done ribs.

Move the ribs from the grill rack, sprinkle with seasoning, cover with foil and leave to rest for 5–10 minutes.

Cut the bones from the ribs, then cut the meat into thick slices. Serve the beef with the aïoli.

MEXICAN TORTILLA WRAPS

PREPARATION TIME 10 minutes, plus 8–24 hours marinating

COOKING TIME 20 minutes

SERVES 6–8

900g/2lb thick piece of skirt, flank or rump steak

MEXICAN HERB MARINADE

2 tbsp olive oil

3 garlic cloves, finely chopped

juice of 1½ limes

½–1 tsp chilli/hot pepper flakes

1 tbsp paprika

1 tsp dried oregano

1 tsp ground cumin

sea salt and freshly ground black pepper

TO SERVE

12–16 tortillas

Roasted Tomato Salsa (see page 157)

1 small Iceberg lettuce, finely shredded

300ml/10fl oz/1¼ cups sour cream

Lay the steak in a non-metallic dish.

Make the marinade by mixing all the ingredients in a blender. Pour over the beef, then cover and leave in a cool place for 8–24 hours, turning occasionally.

Lift the beef from the marinade (reserve the marinade) and cook on an oiled grill rack, basting frequently with the remaining marinade, for about 20 minutes for medium rare. Remove the beef from the rack, cover and leave to rest for about 5 minutes.

Meanwhile, wrap the tortillas in foil and put on the side of the grill rack to warm for 5 minutes.

To serve, slice the beef thinly and serve with the salsa, lettuce, sour cream and tortillas separately so that each person can assemble and roll their own wraps.

WARM BEEF SALAD

PREPARATION TIME 15 minutes, plus 6–8 hours marinating

COOKING TIME 12–20 minutes

SERVES 6

5cm/2in piece fresh root ginger

2 garlic cloves, chopped

150ml/5fl oz/⅔ cup rice wine or dry sherry

2 tbsp crushed Chinese fermented black beans

450g/1lb tail end of fillet of beef

2 tbsp finely chopped coriander/cilantro leaves

1 tbsp rice vinegar or sherry vinegar

1 tbsp groundnut oil

1 tbsp sesame oil

4 handfuls of small spinach leaves, coarsely torn

1 bunch of watercress, coarsely torn

1 small head radicchio, coarsely torn

lightly toasted sesame seeds, to serve

Thinly slice half of the ginger and grate the rest. Cut the slices into shreds and set aside.

Combine the grated ginger with the garlic, rice wine and black beans.

Put the beef into a non-metallic bowl, pour over the ginger mixture, cover and leave in a cool place for 6–8 hours, turning occasionally.

Lift the beef from the marinade (reserve the marinade) and dry it thoroughly. Flatten the thicker end with a rolling pin. Pour the marinade into a pan and bring to the boil on the side of the grill rack until slightly reduced.

Cook the beef on an oiled grill rack, turning and brushing with the marinade occasionally, for 4–8 minutes on each side until done to your liking.

Remove the beef from the grill rack, cover and leave to rest for 5–8 minutes while you strain the marinade into a jug and stir in the coriander/cilantro, rice vinegar, oils and shredded ginger.

Mix the salad leaves in a serving bowl or deep plate. Slice the beef thinly, mix with the sauce and toss with the salad. Scatter over the sesame seeds.

VEAL CHOPS WITH GREEN HERB SAUCE

PREPARATION TIME 10 minutes, plus 2 hours marinating

COOKING TIME 12–15 minutes

SERVES 4

4 veal rib chops, 2.5–4cm/1–1½in thick

2 tbsp extra virgin olive oil

1 tbsp lemon juice

sea salt and freshly ground black pepper

GREEN HERB SAUCE

1 tsp Dijon mustard

120ml/4fl oz/½ cup extra virgin olive oil

1½ tsp lemon juice

3 tbsp chopped flat-leaf parsley leaves

3 tbsp chopped basil leaves

1–2 garlic cloves, crushed

2 tsp small salted capers, well rinsed and dried

Put the veal into a non-metallic dish.

Stir the oil, lemon juice and black pepper together. Pour over the veal and turn the chops over to ensure they are coated thoroughly and evenly. Cover and leave to marinate in a cool place for 2 hours, turning occasionally.

Meanwhile, make the green herb sauce by whisking the mustard, olive oil and lemon juice together until emulsified. Stir in the herbs, garlic and capers, and season to taste. Add more lemon juice, if necessary.

Lift the veal from the dish and cook on an oiled grill rack, turning once, for 12–15 minutes until browned on the outside but still moist and slightly pink inside. Remove from the grill rack, sprinkle with sea salt and serve with the sauce.

VENISON WITH FRESH FIG CHUTNEY

PREPARATION TIME 15 MINUTES, PLUS 2 HOURS MARINATING

COOKING TIME 12–15 MINUTES

SERVES 4

4 venison steaks, 175g/6oz each
½ tsp Chinese five-spice powder
2 tbsp balsamic vinegar
1½ tsp clear honey
freshly ground black pepper

FRESH FIG CHUTNEY
2 tsp olive oil
4 shallots, quartered
pinch of cayenne pepper
2 tbsp port
1 tbsp redcurrant jelly
6 ripe figs, quartered
sea salt and freshly ground black pepper

Season the venison liberally with black pepper, then rub in the five-spice powder. Mix the balsamic vinegar with the honey and brush liberally over the steaks. Cover and leave in a cool place for 2 hours.

Meanwhile, make the chutney by heating the oil in a pan, adding the shallots and cooking gently until softened but not coloured. Stir in the cayenne, then add the port and redcurrant jelly. Bring to the boil, then simmer gently until syrupy. Add the figs and season to taste. Heat through, then remove from the heat and leave to cool.

Cook the venison on an oiled grill rack for about 4 minutes on each side, or until cooked to your liking. Serve with the fig chutney.

FISH & SHELLFISH

Cooking on a grill rack over a high heat is ideal for fish as the intense heat improves the flavour by charring the surface. The most suitable fish are firm species such as cod, haddock, monkfish and swordfish, and oily types like tuna, salmon and sardines. Salmon is best served a little translucent, while tuna is best a little on the rare side, but if you prefer them cooked through, remove from the grill just before the inside is opaque so they continue to cook off the heat.

Fish steaks should be more than 2.5cm/1in thick so that they will not cook too quickly. Cook fish on the highest notch of the grill. The exception is oily fish which should be cooked over a brisk heat close to the fire until the skin is crisp. Allow 10 minutes per 2.5cm/1in thickness of fish, but do keep an eye on it as it can quickly overcook. Delicate white fish, such as lemon sole and plaice, and thin fillets are difficult to barbecue because they disintegrate when you try to turn them. Large fish are easier to handle if cooked in a double-sided hinged fish grilling basket. They can also be wrapped in foil although they will lose some of the characteristic barbecued flavour.

Shellfish are ideal for barbecueing – it is difficult to make a barbecue too hot for them as by the time you char the exterior they are invariably done to perfection. They are best grilled with the shells on to retain their juices and keep them moist.

SEAFOOD KEBABS WITH DILL

PREPARATION TIME 10 minutes, plus 1 hour marinating

COOKING TIME 6–8 minutes

SERVES 4

450g/1lb skinned cod fillet, cut into
2.5cm/1in cubes

16 raw king prawns/jumbo shrimp,
peeled but tails left on

1½ limes, sliced

2 small courgettes/zucchini, sliced diagonally

16 large cherry tomatoes

LIME MARINADE

4 tbsp virgin olive oil

1 tbsp white wine vinegar

juice of ½ lime

2 garlic cloves, crushed

2 tbsp chopped dill

sea salt and freshly ground black pepper

DILL TARTARE DIP

150ml/5fl oz/⅔ cup sour cream

2 tbsp tartare sauce

2 tbsp Mayonnaise (see page 154)

1 tsp chopped dill

Make the marinade by combining the ingredients.

Thread the cod, prawns/shrimp, lime slices, courgettes/zucchini and cherry tomatoes alternately onto eight skewers. Lay them in a shallow, non-metallic dish and pour over the marinade. Turn the kebabs to coat them in the marinade, cover and leave in a cool place for 1 hour, turning occasionally.

Meanwhile, make the dip by mixing all the ingredients together. Season to taste. Cover and chill.

Lift the kebabs from the marinade (reserve any remaining marinade) and cook on an oiled grill rack for about 6–8 minutes, turning occasionally and brushing with the marinade, until the prawns/shrimp have turned pink and the fish is cooked. Serve with the dip.

COD WITH SPICED ORANGE MARINADE

PREPARATION TIME 10 minutes, plus 2–3 hours marinating

COOKING TIME 8–10 minutes

SERVES 4

4 cod steaks, 175g/6oz each, 2.5cm/1in thick

chopped fennel herb, for garnish

lime wedges, to serve

SPICED ORANGE MARINADE

4 tbsp orange juice

4 tbsp dry vermouth

4 tbsp hoisin sauce

4 tbsp soy sauce

1 garlic clove, crushed

½ tsp ground cumin

½ tsp Chinese five-spice powder

freshly ground black pepper

Lay the cod in a shallow, non-metallic dish just large enough to hold the steaks.

Make the marinade by mixing all the ingredients together. Pour over the cod, turn the steaks to ensure they are evenly coated, then cover the dish and leave in a cool place for 2–3 hours.

Lift the cod from the marinade (reserve the marinade) and cook on an oiled grill for 4–5 minutes on each side, brushing occasionally with the marinade. Serve garnished with fennel and accompanied by lime wedges.

PIZZA-STYLE FISH PARCELS

PREPARATION TIME 10 minutes

COOKING TIME 20–25 minutes

SERVES 4

227g/8oz can chopped Italian plum tomatoes

1 garlic clove, finely chopped

pinch of crushed chilli/hot pepper flakes

2 tbsp coarsely chopped basil leaves

4 firm white fish fillets, such as Icelandic cod or haddock, 175g/6oz each

150g/5oz mozzarella cheese, coarsely grated

1 pepperoni sausage, thinly sliced

2 tbsp capers, drained

25g/1oz/⅓ cup freshly grated Parmesan cheese

freshly ground black pepper

Cook the tomatoes, garlic and chilli/hot pepper flakes in a small saucepan over a low heat for 10–12 minutes until most of the liquid has evaporated and the tomatoes are pulpy. Stir in the basil.

Cut four pieces of heavy-duty foil large enough to enclose each fish fillet completely. Place a fillet on each piece of foil and spread one quarter of the tomato mixture over each fillet. Top with the mozzarella, sausage, capers and then the Parmesan. Sprinkle with black pepper and fold the foil loosely over the fish, twisting the edges together firmly to seal them.

Cook on a grill rack for about 10 minutes, turning over halfway through. Just before the end of the cooking time, carefully open one package to check if the flesh flakes easily when tested with the point of a knife.

MAHI MAHI WITH CAPERS AND LEMON

PREPARATION TIME 10 minutes, plus 1 hour marinating

COOKING TIME 6–8 minutes

SERVES 4

4 mahi mahi steaks, or other firm fish steaks, 200g/7oz each

1 tsp chopped thyme leaves, plus extra to serve

1 tsp chopped tarragon leaves, plus extra to serve

2 garlic cloves, finely chopped

sea salt and freshly ground black pepper

2 tbsp olive oil

200ml/7fl oz/¾ cup dry white wine

lemon wedges, to serve

LEMON AND CAPER SAUCE

2 tbsp capers in wine vinegar, drained

juice of 2 small lemons

1 tsp grated lemon zest

5 tbsp olive oil

Lay the fish in a single layer in a non-metallic dish. Sprinkle over the herbs, garlic and seasoning. Pour over the oil and wine, cover and leave in a cool place for 1 hour, turning a couple of times.

Meanwhile, make the sauce by briefly mixing the capers, lemon juice and zest in a small blender or food processor. With the motor running, slowly pour in the oil. Season to taste.

Lift the fish from the dish and cook, skin-side down first, in an oiled fish basket or on an oiled grill for about 3–4 minutes on each side until the flesh flakes easily when tested with the point of a sharp knife. Transfer to plates, pour over the sauce and serve with the lemon wedges and chopped herbs.

HERBED FISH BURGERS

PREPARATION TIME 15 minutes

COOKING TIME 8–10 minutes

SERVES 4

350g/12oz haddock fillet, skinned

1–2 tbsp lemon juice

1 tbsp Worcestershire sauce

1 tsp creamed horseradish

120ml/4fl oz/½ cup milk

1 tbsp snipped chives

1 tbsp chopped parsley leaves

350g/12oz cooked potatoes, mashed with a little butter

50g/2oz/1 cup fresh breadcrumbs

Put the fish, lemon juice, Worcestershire sauce, horseradish and milk in a food processor or blender and mix until smooth. Transfer to a bowl and mix in the herbs and mashed potatoes until evenly combined.

Shape into four equal size burgers. Coat evenly in the breadcrumbs.

Cook the fish burgers in an oiled hinged fish basket for 4–5 minutes on each side until golden and crisp. Alternatively, cook the burgers on an oiled grill rack and turn carefully with a fish slice.

SEA BASS WITH SAUCE VIÈRGE

PREPARATION TIME 10 minutes, plus
   20 minutes marinating

COOKING TIME 6 minutes

SERVES 4

4 sea bass fillets with skin on, 175g/6oz each
olive oil, for brushing
sea salt and freshly ground black pepper

SAUCE VIÈRGE
6 Italian vine-ripened plum tomatoes, finely diced
2 garlic cloves, finely chopped
3 small shallots, finely chopped
sea salt
150ml/5fl oz/⅔ cup extra virgin olive oil
1 tsp lemon juice
3 tbsp shredded basil leaves
freshly ground black pepper

Make the sauce by putting the tomatoes, garlic and shallots in a bowl, sprinkling with a little sea salt and leaving for 20 minutes until the juices run. Add the extra virgin olive oil, lemon juice, basil, and black pepper to taste.

Brush the sea bass with olive oil and sprinkle with seasoning. Cook the fish in an oiled fish basket or on an oiled grill rack, skin-side down first, for 3 minutes, then turn over and cook the other side until the flesh is cooked through.

Remove the fish to plates and spoon over the sauce.

BLACKENED SEA BASS

PREPARATION TIME 10 minutes

COOKING TIME 6 minutes

SERVES 4

4 sea bass fillets with skin on, 175g/6oz each
3½ tbsp unsalted butter, melted
Avocado, Tomato and Red Pepper Salsa
   (see page 158), to serve
lime wedges, to serve

SPICE RUB
1½ tbsp paprika
2 tsp garlic granules
½ tsp dried oregano
½ tsp dried thyme
½ tsp cayenne pepper
sea salt and freshly ground black pepper

Make the spice rub by mixing all the ingredients together and spread on a plate.

Brush the fish with melted butter, then press both sides onto the spice rub, making sure it adheres.

Cook the fish, flesh-side down first, in an oiled fish basket or on an oiled grill rack for 3 minutes. Turn the fish over and cook for a further 3 minutes until the skin is blistered and browned. Serve with salsa and lime wedges.

RED SNAPPER WITH SESAME, GINGER AND CORIANDER

PREPARATION TIME 10 minutes, plus 1–2 hours marinating

COOKING TIME 14 minutes

SERVES 6

120ml/4fl oz/½ cup groundnut oil

1 tbsp sesame oil

1 tbsp soy sauce

juice of 1 lime

2 tbsp rice wine vinegar

1cm/½in piece fresh root ginger, grated

leaves from a small bunch of coriander/cilantro, chopped

6 red snapper or other whole fish, 450g/1lb each, cleaned

sea salt and cracked black pepper

sesame seeds, to serve

Combine the groundnut and sesame oils with the soy sauce, lime juice, vinegar, ginger, coriander/cilantro, salt and black pepper.

Cut two diagonal slashes in each side of the fish and place in a non-metallic dish. Pour the oil mixture over the fish, turn the snappers to coat them evenly, then cover and leave in a cool place for 1–2 hours, turning occasionally.

Cook the snappers in an oiled hinged fish basket for about 7 minutes until the underside is blistered and brown. Turn the fish over and cook on the other side for a further 7 minutes until the flesh near the head flakes easily when tested with the point of a sharp knife. Remove the fish to plates, sprinkle over the sesame seeds and serve.

RED SNAPPER WITH BARBECUE SAUCE

PREPARATION TIME 5 minutes

COOKING TIME 6 minutes

SERVES 4

4 red snapper fillets with skin on, 175g/6oz each

olive oil, for brushing

sea salt and freshly ground black pepper

BARBECUE SAUCE

1–2 garlic cloves, crushed

leaves from a sprig of mint, chopped

1 tbsp sun-dried tomato purée/paste

1 tbsp white wine vinegar

1 tsp Dijon mustard

pinch of caster/granulated sugar

150ml/5fl oz/⅔ cup olive oil

Make the barbecue sauce by putting the garlic, mint, tomato purée/paste, vinegar, mustard and a pinch of sugar into a small blender or food processor. Mix together and then, with the motor running, slowly pour in the oil until completely amalgamated. Season to taste.

Brush the red snapper with oil. Cook in an oiled hinged fish basket or on an oiled grill rack for 3 minutes on each side until the flesh is opaque. Transfer to plates and serve with the sauce.

MONKFISH BROCHETTES WITH ROSEMARY AND ANCHOVY

PREPARATION TIME 10 minutes

COOKING TIME 6–8 minutes

SERVES 4

2 monkfish fillets, about 350g/12oz each, cut into 3cm/1¼in cubes

sea salt and freshly ground black pepper

olive oil, for brushing

lemon wedges, to serve

ROSEMARY AND ANCHOVY SAUCE

1½ tbsp chopped rosemary leaves

9 salted anchovy fillets, rinsed and dried

100ml/3½fl oz/generous ⅓ cup extra virgin olive oil

juice of 1½ lemons

Make the sauce by putting the rosemary into a small blender and chopping finely. Add the anchovy fillets and mix to a thick paste. With the motor running, slowly pour in the oil, then add the lemon juice. Season to taste. Set aside.

Thread the monkfish onto skewers. Season them and brush with oil. Cook on an oiled grill rack for about 6–8 minutes until evenly browned, turning once.

Serve with the sauce and lemon wedges.

FISH TORTILLAS WITH TOMATO
AND CORIANDER SALSA

PREPARATION TIME 15 minutes

COOKING TIME 6 minutes

SERVES 4

1 garlic clove, crushed

sea salt and freshly ground black pepper

½ tsp ground cumin

½ tsp dried oregano

½ tsp hot paprika

1 tbsp lime juice

2 tbsp olive oil

4 flounder fillets, with skin on, 175g/6oz each

8 tortilla wraps

8 tbsp Mayonnaise (see page 154)

TOMATO SALSA

4 vine-ripened tomatoes, deseeded and diced

1 small red onion, finely chopped

2 tbsp chopped coriander/cilantro leaves

1 red chilli, deseeded and finely chopped

1 tbsp lemon juice

Make the salsa by combing the ingredients. Cover and set aside.

Crush the garlic to a paste and mix with a pinch of salt. Combine with the black pepper, spices, lime juice and olive oil. Brush the fish with the mixture.

Cook the fish in an oiled hinged fish basket or on an oiled grill rack for 3 minutes on each side.

Meanwhile, warm the tortillas on the side of the grill rack for 30 seconds on each side. (Wrap in a napkin and keep warm, if necessary.)

Remove the fish from the grill rack or basket, flake it coarsely with a fork and serve in the tortillas with the salsa and a tablespoonful of mayonnaise.

TUNA WITH TOMATOES, MINT AND BASIL

PREPARATION TIME 10 minutes

COOKING TIME 35 minutes

SERVES 4

2 very ripe beefsteak tomatoes

5 tbsp extra virgin olive oil

2 tbsp soy sauce

2 tbsp lemon juice

1 garlic clove, finely chopped

2 tsp finely chopped mint leaves

25g/1oz basil leaves, shredded

cracked black pepper

4 tuna fillets, 200g/7oz each

olive oil, for brushing

sea salt and freshly ground black pepper

Cut the tomatoes into 5cm/2in cubes. Mix with the extra virgin olive oil, soy sauce, lemon juice, garlic, mint, basil and black pepper in a small saucepan and warm gently for 30 minutes.

Brush the tuna with olive oil and sprinkle with seasoning. Grill, skin-side down, on an oiled grill rack for about 2 minutes, then turn over and cook the other side until the flesh is barely cooked, or slightly longer if you don't like the fish too rare. Remove to plates.

Stir the sauce and spoon over the tuna.

TERIYAKI TUNA

PREPARATION TIME 5 minutes, plus 1–2 hours marinating

COOKING TIME 4 minutes

SERVES 4

4 tuna steaks, 175g/6oz each

lightly toasted sesame seeds, lightly crushed, to serve

TERIYAKI MARINADE

2 tbsp mirin

2 tbsp soy sauce

2 tbsp saké

2 tsp grated fresh root ginger

1 garlic clove, crushed through a garlic press

½–¾ tsp Sichuan peppercorns, ground

Lay the tuna in a non-metallic dish.

Make the marinade by mixing all the ingredients together. Pour over the tuna, turn the steaks over to make sure they are evenly coated, then cover and leave in a cool place for 1–2 hours, turning occasionally.

Lift the steaks from the marinade. Reserve the marinade.

Cook the tuna on an oiled grill rack for about 2 minutes, brush with the reserved marinade, turn the steaks over, brush again with the marinade and cook for a further 2 minutes, or until cooked to your liking. Serve the tuna with the sesame seeds sprinkled over.

SICILIAN RED MULLET

PREPARATION TIME 15 minutes

COOKING TIME 12–14 minutes

SERVES 4

4 red mullet, 350g/12oz each, cleaned

olive oil, for brushing

1 tsp fennel seeds

½ tsp cumin seeds

1 tsp dried oregano

½ tsp black peppercorns

1 lemon, quartered and thinly sliced

12 fresh bay leaves

sea salt

Using a sharp knife, cut three deep slashes on each side of all the fish. Brush them with olive oil.

Using a pestle and mortar, crush the fennel, cumin and oregano with the peppercorns.

Rub into the fish, making sure the mixture goes into the slashes. Push a lemon slice and bay leaf into each slash. Brush the fish again with oil and sprinkle with sea salt.

Cook in an oiled fish basket or on an oiled grill rack for 6–7 minutes on each side until cooked through, turning once.

SWORDFISH WITH THYME AND ANISE

PREPARATION TIME 10 minutes, plus
   1–2 hours marinating

COOKING TIME 6 minutes

SERVES 4

4 swordfish steaks, about 200g/7oz each

MARINADE

2 tsp fennel seeds

3 tbsp Pernod

2 tbsp olive oil

2 tsp thyme leaves

1 tsp chilli/hot pepper flakes

4 sun-dried tomato halves, finely chopped

sea salt

Lay the swordfish in a shallow, non-metallic dish.

Make the marinade by heating a small, heavy frying pan. Add the fennel seeds and heat until they begin to darken. Crush lightly, then mix with the remaining ingredients.

Pour the marinade over the fish, turn the steaks to coat them evenly, then cover and leave in a cool place for 1–2 hours, turning once or twice.

Lift the fish from the marinade and cook on an oiled grill rack for 3 minutes or so on each side so they are still slightly pink in the middle.

GREEK-STYLE SWORDFISH

PREPARATION TIME 5 minutes, plus 30 minutes marinating

COOKING TIME 6 minutes

SERVES 4

4 swordfish steaks, 150g/5oz each
50ml/2fl oz/3½ tbsp Greek extra virgin olive oil
juice of ½ lemon
1 tsp dried oregano
sea salt and freshly ground black pepper

Lay the fish in a single layer in a non-metallic dish.

Combine the remaining ingredients. Pour over the fish, turn the steaks over to make sure they are evenly coated, then cover and leave in a cool place for 30 minutes

Lift the steaks from the marinade. Reserve any remaining marinade.

Cook the swordfish in an oiled hinged fish basket or on an oiled grill rack for 3 minutes, brushing with the reserved marinade, then turn the steaks over and cook for a further 3 minutes.

MOROCCAN SPICED HALIBUT

PREPARATION TIME 10 minutes, plus
30–60 minutes marinating (optional)

COOKING TIME 8–10 minutes

SERVES 4

3½ tbsp olive oil

2 tbsp lemon juice

3 garlic cloves, crushed

2 tbsp chopped coriander/cilantro leaves

1 tbsp chopped parsley leaves

1 tbsp chopped mint leaves

1 tsp harissa

1 tsp ground cumin

pinch of saffron threads, lightly toasted and
pounded

4 halibut steaks, 200g/7oz each, 2.5cm/
1in thick

lime wedges, to serve

Combine all the ingredients, except the fish and
lime wedges.

Lay the fish in a single layer in a non-metallic
dish, pour over the marinade and turn the fillets
to ensure they are evenly coated. If liked, cover
and leave in a cool place for 30–60 minutes,
turning occasionally.

Lift the fish from the marinade and cook in an
oiled fish basket or on an oiled grill rack for
4–5 minutes on each side, turning halfway,
until cooked through. Serve with lime wedges.

SEA BREAM WITH FIVE-SPICE POWDER, LIME AND GINGER

PREPARATION TIME 10 minutes, plus 1 hour
marinating

COOKING TIME 20–25 minutes

SERVES 4

2 shallots, chopped

2.5cm/1in piece fresh root ginger, chopped

1 tbsp Chinese five-spice powder

1 tbsp soy sauce

grated zest and juice of 2 limes

2 sea bream, 675g/1½lb each, cleaned

Put the shallots and ginger into a blender and mix
to a paste. Add the five-spice powder, soy sauce,
lime zest and juice and mix briefly.

With a sharp knife, cut two slashes in both sides
of each fish, going right through to the bone.

Brush the five-spice paste over the fish, making
sure it goes well into the slashes. Cover and leave
in a cool place for 1 hour.

Cook the sea bream in an oiled fish basket or
on an oiled grill rack for 20–25 minutes, turning
halfway through the cooking time.

SALMON WITH SPICED TEA MARINADE

PREPARATION TIME 10 minutes plus 2½ hours cooling and marinating

COOKING TIME 8 minutes

SERVES 4

2 Assam teabags

200ml/7fl oz/generous ¾ cup boiling water

6cm/2¼in piece fresh root ginger

4 tbsp sweet soy sauce

1 tbsp clear honey

1 plump garlic clove, peeled

4 pieces salmon fillet with skin on

sesame oil, for brushing

spring onions/scallions, sliced on the diagonal, to serve

Put the teabags into a bowl, pour over boiling water, stir once, then leave to infuse for 5 minutes.

Lift out and discard the teabags. Press the ginger through a garlic press into the tea, then repeat with the garlic. Stir in the soy sauce and honey. Leave until cold.

Put the salmon fillets into a dish in a single layer. Pour over the tea marinade. Turn the salmon over, then cover and leave in a cool place for 2 hours, turning occasionally.

Lift the salmon from the marinade and pat dry. Brush with sesame oil, then cook on an oiled grill rack, skin-side down first, for about 4 minutes on each side until cooked to your liking. Remove the salmon from the grill rack, scatter over the spring onions/scallions and serve.

SALMON OLIVES WITH GREEN HERB SAUCE

PREPARATION TIME 15 minutes

COOKING TIME 20–25 minutes

SERVES 6

3 garlic cloves, unpeeled

olive oil, for brushing

6 pieces salmon tail fillet, 300g/10oz each, skinned

50g/2oz/1 cup dry breadcrumbs

finely grated zest of 3 limes

3 tbsp chopped dill

sea salt and freshly ground black pepper

lemon wedges, to serve

SAUCE

6 tbsp extra virgin olive oil

2 tbsp white wine vinegar

2 tbsp chopped parsley leaves

2 tbsp chopped dill

1 tsp Dijon mustard

Preheat the oven to 200°C/400°F/Gas 6. Brush the garlic cloves with olive oil, place in an ovenproof dish and bake for about 10 minutes until soft. Allow to cool a little.

Meanwhile, make the herb sauce by mixing all the ingredients with seasoning in a blender until smooth. Set aside.

Cut each piece of salmon in half horizontally. Place each piece in turn between two pieces of clingfilm/plastic wrap and beat out carefully with a rolling pin until increased in size by about a quarter.

Peel the cooked garlic and mash the cloves, then mix with the breadcrumbs, lime zest, dill and seasoning. Divide among the salmon slices and roll up towards the narrow end. Secure with wooden cocktail sticks/toothpicks that have been soaked in water for 10 minutes.

Brush the salmon rolls with olive oil and cook on an oiled grill rack for about 10–12 minutes, turning occasionally, until just cooked; take care not to overcook. Serve with the herb sauce and lemon wedges.

FRAGRANT WHOLE SALMON

PREPARATION TIME 10 minutes, plus 8 hours marinating
COOKING TIME 15–20 minutes
SERVES 8

2.5kg/5½lb whole salmon, cleaned

lime wedges, coriander/cilantro leaves and sliced spring onions/scallions, to garnish

HONEY AND GINGER MARINADE
175ml/6fl oz/¾ cup rice wine vinegar
175ml/6fl oz/¾ cup soy sauce
3 tbsp clear honey
1 red chilli, deseeded and finely chopped
5 garlic cloves, thinly sliced into slivers
4 whole star anise, lightly crushed
7.5cm/3in piece fresh root ginger, grated

Make the marinade by putting all the ingredients into a blender and mixing to combine well.

Cut three or four diagonal slashes in both sides of the salmon, then lay the fish in a non-metallic dish. Pour over some of the marinade, making sure that it goes into the slashes. Turn the fish over and pour over the remaining marinade, again making sure that it goes into the slashes. Cover and leave in a cool place for 8 hours, turning the fish occasionally.

Transfer the salmon to a large piece of heavy-duty foil, then fold the foil loosely over the fish and twist the edges together firmly to seal completely. Slash the foil at an angle once or twice down each side but be careful not to cut right round.

Cook the fish on the grill rack for 15–20 minutes, turning halfway through, or for longer if the fire begins to cool down.

Serve the salmon garnished with the lime wedges, coriander/cilantro leaves and sliced spring onions/scallions.

SARDINES WITH COURGETTES, LEMON AND DILL

PREPARATION TIME 15 minutes, plus 2 hours chilling

COOKING TIME 12–14 minutes

SERVES 4

8 large or 12 medium sardines, cleaned
4 courgettes/zucchini, sliced thinly lengthways
sea salt and freshly ground black pepper
extra virgin olive oil, for brushing
lemon wedges, to serve

LEMON AND DILL DRESSING
2 tbsp lemon juice
2 tbsp extra virgin olive oil
fine leaves from 3 bushy dill sprigs

Bury the sardines in sea salt. Set aside in a cool place for 2 hours.

Lift the sardines from the salt and brush them clean.

Brush the courgette/zucchini slices with olive oil and barbecue for about 3 minutes on each side until nicely marked. Remove to a serving dish.

Meanwhile, make the dressing by whisking together the lemon juice, oil and seasoning. Add the dill. Trickle over the cooked courgette/zucchini slices and set aside while cooking the sardines.

Brush the sardines with olive oil and sprinkle with black pepper. Put in a hinged fish basket or thread onto pairs of oiled parallel skewers, alternating the heads and tails, and place on an oiled grill rack. Cook lightly on one side for 3–4 minutes, turn them over and cook the other side until the skin is scorched and bubbling. Serve the sardines with the courgettes/zucchini and lemon wedges.

SPICED SARDINES WITH ORANGE AND OLIVE SALAD

PREPARATION TIME 15 minutes, plus 2–3 hours marinating

COOKING TIME 6–8 minutes

SERVES 4

4 garlic cloves, crushed

1 tbsp olive oil

1 tbsp lemon juice

1 tsp ground Sichuan peppercorns

½ tsp hot paprika

12–16 fresh sardines, depending on size, cleaned

sea salt and freshly ground black pepper

ORANGE AND OLIVE SALAD

5 oranges

1 small red onion, very thinly sliced

16 large salt-packed black olives, pitted

25g/1oz flat-leaf parsley leaves, coarsely chopped

extra virgin olive oil, for trickling

Mix together the garlic, olive oil, lemon juice, peppercorns, paprika and seasoning. Rub thoroughly over the sardines, cover and leave in a cool place for 2–3 hours.

Make the salad by peeling and segmenting the oranges, removing all the pith and membranes. Put the segments in a bowl with the red onion, olives and parsley. Season and trickle over some oil.

Cook the sardines in an oiled fish basket or thread them onto pairs of oiled parallel skewers, alternating the heads and tails, and cook on an oiled grill rack for 3–4 minutes on each side. Serve with the orange and olive salad.

MACKEREL WITH SWEET CHILLI AND MINT

PREPARATION TIME 10 minutes, plus 2 hours chilling

COOKING TIME 10 minutes

SERVES 4

4 mackerel, 325g/11oz each, cleaned

sea salt

CHILLI AND MINT DRESSING

3 tbsp rice wine vinegar

2 tbsp caster/granulated sugar

1½ tbsp chopped mint leaves

1 large red chilli, deseeded and finely chopped

5cm/2in piece fresh root ginger, finely chopped

Bury the mackerel in sea salt. Set aside in a cool place for 2 hours.

Lift the mackerel from the salt and brush them clean.

To make the dressing, whisk the vinegar with the sugar, then stir in the remaining ingredients.

Cut two slashes in each side of all the mackerel, going right through to the bone. Season and cook in an oiled hinged fish basket for about 5 minutes. Turn the fish over and cook on the other side for a further 5 minutes until the flesh near the head flakes easily when tested with the point of a sharp knife and the skin is very crisp. Remove to plates and serve with the dressing.

TROUT WITH TARRAGON

PREPARATION TIME 10 minutes, plus 1–2 hours marinating

COOKING TIME 12 minutes

SERVES 4

4 trout, 350g/12oz each, cleaned

TARRAGON MARINADE

5 tbsp extra virgin olive oil

1½ tbsp lemon juice

2 small shallots, finely chopped

1 garlic clove, finely chopped

1½ tsp coarsely chopped tarragon leaves

1½ tsp coarsely chopped flat-leaf parsley leaves

1 tsp Dijon mustard

1 tsp anise, such as Pernod or Ricard

1 tsp dark soy sauce

Using the point of a sharp knife, cut three slashes in both sides of each trout.

Make the marinade by mixing all the ingredients. Brush liberally over the trout and into the slashes. Cover and leave in a cool place for 1–2 hours.

Cook the trout in an oiled fish basket or on an oiled grill rack for about 6 minutes. Turn the fish over (if necessary carefully use a large fish slice), brush liberally with the marinade and cook for a further 6 minutes, or until the flesh near the head flakes easily. Move the fish to the side of the grill rack, if necessary, to ensure even cooking. Transfer to plates and pour over any remaining marinade.

CRAB BURGERS

PREPARATION TIME 10 minutes, plus 1–2 hours chilling

COOKING TIME 6–8 minutes

SERVES 4

1 potato, about 225g/8oz, baked in its skin

small knob unsalted butter

225g/8oz crab meat

1 small red chilli, deseeded and finely chopped

8 plump spring onions/scallions, finely chopped

1 tsp harissa paste

2 tsp Thai fish sauce

1 large egg white, lightly beaten

75–115g/3–4oz polenta

2 tsp sesame seeds

Scoop the flesh from the baked potato and mash it with the small knob of butter. Leave to cool, then mix with the crab meat, chilli, spring onions/scallions, harissa, fish sauce and egg white. Divide the mixture into eight pieces and form into burgers.

Mix the polenta with the sesame seeds, then coat the burgers in the mixture. Chill for 1–2 hours.

Cook the burgers in an oiled hinged fish basket for about 3–4 minutes on each side until they are golden on the outside and warmed through. Alternatively, cook on an oiled grill rack and turn the burgers carefully with a fish slice.

PRAWNS WITH ASIAN PESTO

PREPARATION TIME 10 minutes, plus 1 hour marinating

COOKING TIME 6 minutes

SERVES 4–6

700g/1½lb large raw prawns/shrimps with shells on

ASIAN PESTO

1½–2 tbsp groundnut oil

2 tbsp finely chopped garlic

2 tbsp finely chopped fresh root ginger

2 tbsp finely chopped basil leaves

1½ tbsp finely chopped chilli

2 tsp rice wine

1 tbsp sesame oil

sea salt and freshly ground black pepper

Make the pesto by mixing the ingredients to a paste in a blender.

Remove the legs from the prawns/shrimps, keeping the shells intact. Using the point of a small sharp knife, cut a few slits in the shell of the prawns/shrimps. Rub the pesto thoroughly over the prawns/shrimps and leave in a cool place for 1 hour.

Cook the prawns/shrimps on an oiled grill rack for about 3 minutes on each side until the shells turn pink.

PRAWNS WITH LEMON GRASS AND PAPAYA

PREPARATION TIME 15 minutes, plus 1 hour marinating

COOKING TIME 4–6 minutes

SERVES 4–6

4 lemon grass stems, peeled and finely chopped

1 plump garlic clove, chopped

5 tbsp extra virgin olive oil

1½ limes

1 red chilli, deseeded and chopped

28 raw tiger prawns/shrimp, peeled but tails left on

1 papaya, peeled and halved

4 spring onions/scallions, chopped

handful of coriander/cilantro leaves, finely chopped

sea salt and freshly ground black pepper

lime wedges, to serve

Combine the lemon grass, garlic, 2 tablespoons of the oil, the juice of 1 lime and two-thirds of the chilli in a bowl. Stir in the prawns/shrimps, cover and leave in a cool place for 1 hour.

Meanwhile, scoop the seeds from the papaya and dice the flesh. Mix with the juice of the remaining half lime, the remaining chilli, spring onions/scallions, coriander/cilantro and seasoning.

Lift the prawns/shrimps from the marinade and cook on an oiled grill rack for 2–3 minutes on each side until they turn pink. Serve with the salsa and lime wedges.

PRAWN PINWHEELS

PREPARATION TIME 10 minutes, plus 2 hours marinating

COOKING TIME 5–6 minutes

SERVES 6

24 raw tiger prawns/shrimps

2 tsp cumin seeds

1 tbsp chilli/hot pepper flakes

1 star anise

1 tbsp fenugreek seeds

3 tbsp groundnut oil

4 shallots, chopped

4 garlic cloves, chopped

2 pinches of ground turmeric

sea salt and freshly ground black pepper

lemon wedges, to serve

Remove the heads from the prawns/shrimps and peel the bodies, leaving the tails in place. Put in a shallow, non-metallic dish.

Dry-fry the cumin seeds, chilli/hot pepper flakes and star anise for 1 minute, stirring. Grind finely in a spice grinder, or crush using the end of a rolling pin in a small bowl. Set aside.

Fry the fenugreek seeds in 1 tablespoon of the oil until they start to crackle. Add to the spices.

Put the shallots, garlic, turmeric and remaining oil into a blender and add the spice mixture, salt and plenty of black pepper. Mix to a coarse paste. Spread evenly over the prawns/shrimps. Cover and leave in a cool place for 2 hours.

Curl each prawn/shrimp in a tight spiral, then thread onto an oiled skewer, inserting it at the base of the tail end. Cook on an oiled grill rack for 3–4 minutes, turning once, until pink. Squeeze the lemon over the prawns/shrimps and serve. (If you wish, the lemon wedges can be lightly charred on the barbecue.)

SCALLOPS WITH THAI DIPPING SAUCE

PREPARATION TIME 10 minutes

COOKING TIME 4–6 minutes

SERVES 4

20 scallops

sesame oil, for brushing

20 coriander/cilantro leaves

20 thin slices of pickled ginger

THAI DIPPING SAUCE

2 tbsp Thai fish sauce

1 tbsp lime juice

1 tsp finely chopped garlic

1 tsp finely chopped red chilli

1 spring onion/scallion, thinly sliced

2 tsp finely chopped peanuts

2½ tsp chopped peeled cucumber

1½ tbsp palm sugar or dark brown sugar

Make the dipping sauce by stirring the ingredients together until the sugar has dissolved, then pour into a small serving bowl.

Brush the scallops lightly with sesame oil. Lay them on the grill rack and cook for 2–3 minutes on each side until they just change colour, turning once. Take care not to overcook.

Remove from the rack and pierce each scallop onto a toothpick, adding a coriander/cilantro leaf and a slice of pickled ginger. Serve with the dipping sauce.

BACON-WRAPPED SCALLOP KEBABS

PREPARATION TIME 10 minutes

COOKING TIME 4–6 minutes

SERVES 4

12 large scallops with roes, shucked

6 rashers of streaky bacon, rinds removed

Worcestershire sauce

lemon wedges, to serve

Remove the corals from the scallops and set aside

Stretch the bacon rashers on a chopping board with the back of a knife and cut across into halves. Wrap a piece of bacon around each scallop. Thread three wrapped scallops lengthways onto a soaked bamboo skewer, putting a coral between each one. Repeat with the remaining scallops and corals.

Season the bacon with Worcestershire sauce and cook on an oiled grill rack for 2–3 minutes on each side until the bacon is crisp and the scallops just opaque; take care not to overcook the scallops. Serve immediately, with lemon wedges.

LOBSTER WITH ALMOND, CHEESE AND HERB DRESSING

PREPARATION TIME 15 minutes, plus 20 minutes soaking

COOKING TIME 9 minutes

SERVES 4

2 uncooked lobsters, each 700g–1kg/1½–2¼lb

olive oil, for brushing

lemon wedges, to serve

DRESSING

25g/1oz/scant ¼ cup almonds

6 tbsp chopped flat-leaf parsley leaves

7 tbsp chopped mixed herbs such as chervil, dill, fennel, mint and chives

1 garlic clove, chopped

200ml/7fl oz/generous ¾ cup mild olive oil

40g/1½ oz/⅔ cup freshly grated Parmesan cheese

about 1 tsp lemon juice

sea salt and freshly ground black pepper

Make the dressing by pouring boiling water over the almonds and leaving for 20 minutes. Drain the almonds and remove the skins.

Put the almonds into a blender or food processor. Add all the herbs and garlic. Process until finely chopped. With the motor running, slowly pour in the oil in a thin, steady stream. Add the cheese. Mix briefly, then season with lemon juice, salt and pepper. Transfer to a bowl.

Put the lobsters on a strong board, stomach down, and, using a large sharp knife, slice them in half lengthways. Discard the stomachs and intestines. Crack the claws with the back of the knife, or use a hammer.

Brush the lobster flesh and shells with olive oil. Lay the lobsters, flesh-side down, on a grill rack over a medium-hot fire and cook for 30 seconds. Turn them over and cook for a further 8 minutes or so until the shells have turned bright red and the flesh has become white.

Add a little dressing to each lobster half and serve the rest separately with the lemon wedges.

MUSSELS EN PAPILLOTE WITH COCONUT, GINGER, LEMON AND LIME

PREPARATION TIME 10 minutes

COOKING TIME 10 minutes

SERVES 4

50g/2oz chopped fresh root ginger

2 lemon grass stems, crushed and finely chopped

juice and grated zest of 1 lemon

juice and grated zest of 1 lime

4 garlic cloves, finely chopped

leaves from a small sprig of thyme

sea salt and freshly ground black pepper

1.25kg/2lb 12oz mussels, scrubbed and bearded

200ml/7fl oz/generous ¾ cup coconut milk

In a large bowl mix together the ginger, lemon grass, lemon and lime zests and juices, garlic, thyme and seasoning. Add the mussels and stir thoroughly.

Cut four large pieces of heavy-duty foil and pile a quarter of the mussel mixture onto each one. Trickle the coconut milk evenly over the mussels. Fold the edges of the foil loosely over the mussels and twist the edges firmly together to seal.

Cook on the grill rack for about 10 minutes until all the mussels have opened, turning the packages over a couple of times. Discard any mussels that remain closed. Serve the mussels in their parcels.

SEARED SQUID SALAD

PREPARATION TIME 15 minutes, plus 2–4 hours marinating

COOKING TIME 4 minutes

SERVES 6

900g/2lb small squid, cleaned

CHILLI MARINADE
1 tbsp groundnut oil
1 tsp sesame oil
1 tbsp lemon juice
1 red chilli, deseeded and finely chopped
1 garlic clove, crushed
sea salt

TO SERVE
handful of curly endive
12 cherry tomatoes, quartered
1 bunch watercress, trimmed
½ cucumber, peeled, halved, deseeded and cut into fine strips
groundnut oil and lime juice, for dressing
sea salt and freshly ground black pepper
2–3 tbsp coriander/cilantro leaves

Remove the tentacles from the squid and cut the squid bodies lengthways along one side to open them out flat. Using the point of a knife, score diagonal parallel lines on the squid bodies but do not cut right through. Put into a non-metallic bowl. Leave the tentacles whole and add them to the bowl.

Make the marinade by combining all the ingredients. Pour over the squid, stir everything together, cover and leave to marinate in a cool place for 2–4 hours.

Lift the squid from the marinade and cook on an oiled grill rack for 2 minutes on each side, turning once, until just opaque.

Meanwhile, toss the curly endive, tomatoes, watercress and cucumber together. Trickle over about 2 tablespoons groundnut oil and 1 tablespoon lime juice, to just moisten. Season.

Slice the squid into rings and pile onto the salad. Garnish with fresh coriander/cilantro.

VEGETARIAN DISHES

A selection of grilled vegetable dishes works well as a main course for a barbecue. Add an interesting dressing or sauce, some cheese and bread, cooked or warmed on the grill rack, and a barbecued potato dish to make a delicious spread.

Many vegetables respond well to being barbecued, but some take a surprisingly long time to cook. Pre-cook firm veg such as carrots, cauliflower, baby onions and broccoli in boiling water to reduce the cooking time and to prevent the outside becoming overdone before the inside is tender. Drain and dry them well before cooking on the grill rack. Coat cut surfaces with oil or dressing to prevent them drying and to promote browning. Sweet potatoes and baby squash can be cooked in the embers of the fire. Wrapping them in double-thickness foil keeps them clean and helps them to cook evenly.

When choosing vegetables, bear in mind cooking times. This is particularly important when making kebabs as all the items must cook in the same time, (after any initial cooking for items such as new potatoes and mini fennel bulbs). If cooking vegetables loose, put those that require the longest cooking on first. Use an oiled hinged grill basket because it will make turning and lifting vegetables easier, or try an oiled fine-mesh grill rack which will prevent small items, such as button mushrooms and shallots, falling onto the coals. Vegetables can also be enclosed in foil parcels and cooked on the grill rack for maximum flavour.

VEGETABLE SATAY

PREPARATION TIME 15 minutes

COOKING TIME 30 minutes

SERVES 4

1 small squash, peeled and cut into chunks

2 leeks, cut into chunks

1 courgette/zucchini, cut into chunks

100g/3½oz mushrooms, halved

3 tbsp dark soy sauce

2 tsp sesame oil

8–12 fresh bay leaves

SATAY SAUCE

1 tbsp groundnut oil

1 shallot, finely chopped

2 garlic cloves, crushed

2.5cm/1in piece fresh root ginger, grated

1 stalk lemon grass

1 red chilli, deseeded and finely chopped

1 tsp curry powder

150g/5oz/⅔ cup crunchy peanut butter

3 tbsp chopped coriander/cilantro leaves

sugar, sea salt and freshly ground black pepper

To make the sauce, heat the oil and fry the shallot, garlic, ginger and lemon grass until softened. Stir in the chilli and curry powder for a couple of minutes. Then stir in the peanut butter and 250ml/9fl oz/generous 1 cup boiling water. Bring to the boil, add the coriander/cilantro and season with sugar, salt and pepper. Remove from the heat.

Meanwhile, cook the squash in a pan of boiling water for 5 minutes. Add the leeks and cook for a further 3 minutes. Drain and cool under running cold water. Put into a bowl with the courgette/zucchini and mushrooms.

Combine the soy sauce, sesame oil and black pepper. Trickle over the vegetables and stir gently to coat all the vegetables.

Thread the vegetables alternately onto skewers, adding bay leaves along the way. Cook on an oiled grill rack for about 8 minutes, turning occasionally.

Meanwhile, warm the satay sauce on the side of the grill rack and serve with the vegetables.

SPICED TOFU BURGERS
WITH FRESH CORIANDER CHUTNEY

PREPARATION TIME 20 minutes, plus 2–24 hours marinating

COOKING TIME 15 minutes

SERVES 4

115g/4oz leeks, cut into 5cm/2in lengths

1 stick celery (about 125g/4½oz), grated lengthways

olive oil, for frying

2 garlic cloves, finely chopped

¾ tsp cumin seeds, crushed

2 tsp sun-dried tomato purée/paste

1 tsp curry paste

250g/9oz pack tofu, drained

6 tbsp fresh breadcrumbs

sea salt and freshly ground black pepper

beaten egg

seasoned plain/all-purpose flour, for coating

FRESH CORIANDER/CILANTRO CHUTNEY

40g/1½oz coriander/cilantro leaves, coarsely chopped

2 tsp grated fresh root ginger

1 garlic clove, chopped

2 tsp lime juice

1–2 peppadews (bottled mild sweet piquante peppers) or ½ deseeded red chilli, finely chopped

pinch of sugar

Grate the leeks lengthways and mix with the celery. Using kitchen scissors, cut into shorter pieces.

Heat the oil in a frying pan, add the leeks and celery and fry, stirring, until softened, reduced and lightly coloured, then add the garlic towards the end of cooking. Stir in the cumin, tomato purée/paste and curry paste and cook, stirring, for a couple of minutes. Remove from the heat.

Mash the tofu. Using your hands or a fork, mix the tofu with the vegetable mixture, breadcrumbs, seasoning and a little egg until the mixture holds together; only add just enough egg to bind the mixture. With floured hands, press firmly into eight burgers about 1–2cm/½–¾in thick. Chill, uncovered, for at least 2 hours, or overnight.

Make the chutney by putting the half the coriander/cilantro, the ginger, garlic, lime juice, peppadews and 2 tablespoons of water in a blender and mixing until smooth. Add the remaining coriander/cilantro and mix again, leaving some texture in the leaves. Season to taste with sugar, salt and pepper. Transfer to a small serving bowl, cover and chill for up to 30 minutes.

Cook the burgers on an oiled grill rack for about 4 minutes on each side, turning carefully once, until browned. Serve with the fresh chutney.

VEGETABLE BROCHETTES

PREPARATION TIME 20 minutes, plus 1 hour marinating

COOKING TIME 10 minutes

SERVES 6

1 large aubergine/eggplant, cut into 12 slices

3 red peppers, deseeded and quartered

24 large button mushrooms

3 courgettes/zucchini, scored lengthways with a fork, cut diagonally into 2cm/¾in pieces

175g/6oz halloumi cheese, cut into 2.5 x 1cm/ 1 x ½in pieces

2 tbsp extra virgin olive oil

juice of 1 lime

leaves from a small bunch of fresh coriander/ cilantro, chopped

PAPRIKA MARINADE

3 tbsp soy sauce

1½ tbsp olive oil

2 garlic cloves, crushed

1 tbsp paprika

1 tbsp ground cumin

dash of Tabasco sauce

Make the marinade by combining the ingredients with 3 tablespoons of water. Brush the aubergine/ eggplant slices with some of the marinade.

Put the remaining vegetables in a dish and stir in the remaining marinade. Cover and leave in a cool place for an hour or so.

Meanwhile, cook the aubergine/eggplant slices on an oiled grill rack, or under a preheated grill, for 3–4 minutes until browned, turning once. Grill the halloumi for 2 minutes until golden but not melting. Wrap the aubergine/eggplant slices round the pieces of halloumi.

Remove the vegetables from the marinade. Beginning and ending with a mushroom, thread the vegetables, including the aubergines/ eggplant, alternately onto oiled skewers.

Cook on an oiled grill rack for about 4 minutes, turning to ensure even cooking and browning.

Meanwhile, combine the olive oil, lime juice, coriander/cilantro and seasoning. Remove the brochettes from the grill rack and trickle over the dressing.

MUSHROOM KEBABS

PREPARATION TIME 10 minutes

COOKING TIME 5 minutes

SERVES 2–4

450g/1lb oyster mushrooms

lemon juice

freshly ground black pepper

25g/1oz/2 tbsp unsalted butter, melted

Basil and Grilled Tomato Pesto (see page 154)
    or Tomato Tartare Sauce (see page 156) or
    Sun-dried Tomato and Garlic Mayonnaise
    (see page 155), to serve

Sprinkle the mushrooms with a little lemon juice
and season them with black pepper.

Thread the mushrooms onto oiled skewers and
brush with melted butter.

Cook on an oiled grill rack, turning frequently,
for 5 minutes. Serve with your choice of the
suggested accompaniments.

ASH-BAKED
SWEET POTATO

PREPARATION TIME 5 minutes

COOKING TIME 45 minutes

SERVES 4

4 sweet potatoes, pricked

TO SERVE

Pesto (see page 154), Sun-dried Tomato and
    Garlic Mayonnaise (see page 155),
    Parsley and Lemon Butter (see page 143)
    or unsalted butter

freshly grated Parmesan and black pepper,
    or cottage cheese or ricotta and red pesto

Wrap the sweet potatoes individually in roomy
but well-sealed double-thickness foil parcels.

Cook in the embers of the fire for about
45 minutes or until tender, turning occasionally.

Remove from the fire and serve with the chosen
accompaniment(s).

ASPARAGUS WITH CRISP CRUMB, EGG AND OLIVE GREMOLATA

PREPARATION TIME 10 minutes

COOKING TIME 6 minutes

SERVES 4

450g/1lb slim asparagus*
olive oil, for brushing
50g/2oz/3½ tbsp unsalted butter, diced
25g/1oz/½ cup fresh, coarse breadcrumbs
grated zest of 1 lemon
2 tbsp chopped parsley leaves
50g/2oz/½ cup pitted green olives, chopped
1 large hard-boiled egg, shelled and finely chopped
sea salt and freshly ground black pepper
lemon wedges, to serve

Trim the tough ends from the asparagus spears. Brush with olive oil and cook on a grill rack, turning halfway through, for about 6 minutes until tender and lightly charred. Take care that the spears do not become over-charred.

Meanwhile, to make the gremolata, heat the butter in a heavy-based frying pan, add the breadcrumbs and fry until crisp and golden, stirring frequently. Remove from the heat and stir in the lemon zest, parsley, olives and seasoning.

Transfer the asparagus to a plate, or plates and season. Scatter the crumb mixture and chopped egg evenly over the spears, leaving the tips uncovered. Serve with lemon wedges.

* If only fatter asparagus spears are available, pare off the tougher skin from the lower parts of the stalks using a potato peeler. Par-boil the spears in boiling water, drain and dry well before brushing with the oil.

GRILLED BABY AUBERGINES WITH MOROCCAN TOPPING

PREPARATION TIME 10 minutes

COOKING TIME 4–6 minutes

SERVES 4

8 baby aubergines/eggplants
olive oil, for brushing
sea salt and freshly ground black pepper

MOROCCAN TOPPING
about 2 tbsp extra virgin olive oil
1½ tsp harissa paste
1 plump garlic clove, finely chopped
1 tsp cumin seeds, toasted and ground
1½ tsp paprika
4 small vine-ripened plum tomatoes,
finely chopped
sea salt and freshly ground black pepper
a pinch of sugar
1 tbsp chopped coriander/cilantro leaves

Make the topping by combining the olive oil and harissa, then mix in the garlic, cumin seeds and paprika. Stir in the tomatoes and salt and pepper, and a pinch of sugar to taste, if necessary. Cover and set aside until required.

Halve the aubergines/eggplants lengthways, leaving the stalk on. Brush with olive oil and sprinkle with seasoning. Cook cut-side down on an oiled grill rack over a medium-high heat, until browned in patches. Turn over and cook for a further 2–3 minutes until tender.

Pile the topping onto the hot aubergine/eggplant halves. Sprinkle over the chopped coriander/cilantro. Transfer to a serving dish and serve warm or cold.

AUBERGINE AND MOZZARELLA ROLLS

PREPARATION TIME 15 minutes, plus 30–60 minutes draining

COOKING TIME 6–8 minutes

SERVES 4–6

2 aubergines/eggplants

sea salt and freshly ground black pepper

1 tbsp extra virgin olive oil, plus extra for brushing

120g/4oz Pesto (see page 154)

12 oil-cured black olives, pitted and cut into slivers

6 sun-dried tomatoes in oil, drained and sliced

3 tbsp shredded basil leaves

150g/5oz buffalo mozzarella, diced

15g/½oz Parmesan, freshly grated

Cut each aubergine/eggplant into six lengthways slices, 5mm/¼in thick. Sprinkle salt over the slices and leave to drain for 30–60 minutes. Rinse off the salt and dry the slices thoroughly.

Brush the slices with extra virgin olive oil and cook on an oiled grill rack for 2–3 minutes on each side until lightly charred and softened, turning once. Remove from the grill.

Using half of the pesto, spread a little over each aubergine/eggplant slice. Scatter with olives, sun-dried tomatoes, basil and mozzarella. Sprinkle with black pepper.

Roll up the aubergine/eggplant slices, starting at a short end. Secure with soaked wooden cocktail sticks/toothpicks. Sprinkle over the Parmesan and return to the oiled grill rack for about 2 minutes on each side until warmed through and lightly golden.

Meanwhile, mix the tablespoon of extra virgin olive oil with the remaining pesto. Transfer the aubergine/eggplant rolls to plates, spoon over the pesto dressing and serve immediately.

GREEK VEGETABLE SALAD

PREPARATION TIME 15 minutes, plus 1 hour marinating

COOKING TIME 20–30 minutes

SERVES 4

225g/8oz feta cheese, cut into 1cm/
  ½in thick slices

120ml/4fl oz/½ cup extra virgin olive oil

grated zest and juice of 1½ lemons

1 tbsp balsamic vinegar

2 garlic cloves, finely chopped

2–3 tbsp thyme leaves

freshly ground black pepper

1.3kg/3lb mixed aubergines/eggplants,
  courgettes/zucchini, ripe but not soft
  tomatoes, and 1 red onion

115g/4oz/heaped 1 cup pitted kalamata olives

Put the cheese into a shallow, non-metallic dish. Combine 2 tablespoons of the olive oil with the lemon zest and juice, balsamic vinegar, garlic, 1 tablespoon of the thyme, and black pepper. Pour over the cheese and leave in a cool place to marinate for 1 hour.

Meanwhile, cut the aubergines/eggplants and courgettes/zucchini diagonally into 1cm/½in thick slices. Halve the tomatoes. Cut the red onion into 1cm/½in slices from top to bottom. Put the courgettes/zucchini, aubergines/eggplants and red onion into a bowl, pour over the remaining oil, add black pepper and stir to coat the vegetables well.

Lift the vegetables from the bowl with a slotted spoon and cook on an oiled grill rack for 5–6 minutes on each side until tender and lightly charred.

Meanwhile, brush the tomatoes with the oil. Cook on the grill rack for 3 minutes on each side.

Transfer the vegetables as they are done to a bowl or platter and cover with clingfilm/plastic wrap.

Lift the cheese from the marinade and cook on the grill rack for about 3 minutes on each side until golden (feta cheese is easier to turn on the grill rack if it is cooked in an oiled hinged basket).

Scatter the olives and remaining thyme over the vegetables and top with the cheese. Serve immediately, while the cheese is still warm.

SPICED LENTIL BURGERS

PREPARATION TIME 15 minutes, plus 1 hour chilling

COOKING TIME 45–50 minutes

SERVES 4

225g/8oz/1¼ cups green or brown lentils
2 large onions, finely chopped
2 carrots, finely chopped
1 celery stick, finely chopped
olive oil, for frying
2 garlic cloves, finely chopped
1 tsp ground cumin
1 tsp ground coriander
3 tbsp chopped parsley leaves
3 tbsp chopped coriander/cilantro leaves
1 tbsp lemon juice
sea salt and freshly ground black pepper
seasoned plain/all-purpose flour, for coating
Avocado, Tomato and Red Pepper Salsa
(see page 158)

Cook the lentils in boiling unsalted water for about 20–30 minutes until tender. Drain well and leave to cool.

Fry the onion, carrot and celery in a little olive oil for 10 minutes until soft and lightly browned. Stir in the lentils, garlic, spices, herbs, lemon juice and seasoning. Mix to a coarse purée in a food processor until the mixture holds together. Alternatively, mash with a potato masher.

With floured hands, form into 12 flat burgers about 1–2cm/½–¾in thick. Coat the burgers in seasoned flour and pat in gently. Cover and chill for at least 1 hour to firm up, or overnight, if possible, to allow the flavours to develop.

Cook in an oiled grill basket, on an oiled mesh grill or on an oiled grill rack, turning once, for 6–8 minutes until crisp and browned. Serve with the avocado, tomato and red pepper salsa.

FALAFEL BURGERS
WITH YOGURT AND MINT RELISH

PREPARATION TIME 10 minutes, plus 2 hours chilling

COOKING TIME 10 minutes

SERVES 4–6

2 x 400g/14oz cans chickpeas,
drained and rinsed

1 garlic clove, chopped

2 tbsp tahini

1 tsp ground cumin

1 tsp ground coriander

50g/2oz/1 cup fresh breadcrumbs

3 tbsp chopped coriander/cilantro leaves

sea salt and freshly ground black pepper

seasoned plain/all-purpose flour, for coating

pitta bread and lettuce leaves, to serve

YOGURT AND MINT RELISH

1 small garlic clove, peeled

sea salt and freshly ground black pepper

150ml/5fl oz/²⁄₃ cup Greek yogurt

4 tbsp chopped mint leaves

a dash of Tabasco sauce

small sprig of mint leaves, to garnish

Put all the burger ingredients except the plain flour into a food processor and mix until the chickpeas are finely chopped, but do not let the mixture turn to a purée.

Transfer to a bowl and stir in about 2 tablespoons of water, kneading until the mixture holds together. With well-floured hands, form the mixture into eight burgers about 2.5cm/1in thick. Chill for at least 2 hours.

To make the relish, crush the garlic with a pinch of salt, then mix it with the yogurt. Add the mint, and season with Tabasco and black pepper, to taste. Chill before serving. Garnish with the mint leaves to serve.

Cook the burgers in an oiled grill basket, on an oiled mesh grill or on an oiled grill rack for about 5 minutes on each side until crisp and brown on the outside and warmed through.

Meanwhile, warm the pitta breads on the side of the grill rack for 30 seconds on each side.

Split the pitta breads open, add the falafel and top with the lettuce, and yogurt and mint relish.

COURGETTE BURGERS WITH DILL TZATZIKI

  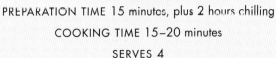

PREPARATION TIME 15 minutes, plus 2 hours chilling

COOKING TIME 15–20 minutes

SERVES 4

500g/1lb 2oz small courgettes/zucchini, grated

175g/6oz/3 cups fresh breadcrumbs

2 eggs, lightly beaten

6 spring onions/scallions, very finely chopped

1 heaped tbsp chopped mint leaves

2 heaped tbsp chopped parsley leaves

sea salt and freshly ground black pepper

4 ciabatta rolls, split into halves

DILL TZATZIKI

400ml/14fl oz/scant 2 cups sheep's milk yogurt

2 tbsp chopped dill leaves

Layer the courgettes/zucchini and a good sprinkling of salt in a colander. Leave for 30–60 minutes.

Meanwhile, preheat the oven to 190°C/375°F/ Gas 5. Reserve 4 tablespoons of the breadcrumbs and spread the remainder on a baking sheet. Bake for 10 minutes, stirring occasionally, until brown and crisp. Spread on a plate and set aside to cool.

Rinse the courgettes/zucchini thoroughly, squeeze firmly to expel as much water as possible, then pat dry between two clean dish towels.

Mix the courgettes/zucchini with the reserved breadcrumbs, the eggs, spring onions/scallions,

herbs and black pepper. With floured hands, form into 18 burgers about 1–2cm/½–¾in thick. Coat evenly and thoroughly in the toasted breadcrumbs, and press the breadcrumbs in. Leave uncovered in the refrigerator for 1 hour or so.

Make the tzatziki by beating the yogurt until smooth, then stir in the dill and seasoning.

Cook the burgers on an oiled grill rack, preferably using an oiled fine mesh grill or hinged wire basket, for about 3–4 minutes until browned and crisp underneath, then turn carefully and cook on the other side.

Meanwhile, lightly toast the rolls on the side of the grill rack. Serve the burgers in the rolls with the tzatziki spooned on top.

HALLOUMI, SQUASH AND CHERRY TOMATO SKEWERS

PREPARATION TIME 5 minutes, plus 2–24 hours marinating

COOKING TIME 10 minutes

SERVES 4

350g/12oz halloumi cheese, cut into 2.5cm/
1in cubes

16 small patty pan squash

16 cherry tomatoes, preferably plum

HERB MARINADE

6 tbsp extra virgin olive oil

2 tbsp mixed chopped oregano, thyme, mint,
rosemary and parsley leaves

juice of 1 lemon

freshly ground black pepper

Put the cheese and vegetables into a shallow, non-metallic dish.

Make the marinade by mixing all the ingredients together. Pour over the cheese and vegetable mixture, then stir to make sure everything is coated. Cover and leave in a cool place for at least 2 hours and up to 24 hours.

Lift the cheese and vegetables from the marinade (reserve any remaining marinade) and thread alternately onto skewers, beginning and ending with a patty pan squash and pushing all the ingredients quite closely together.

Cook on an oiled grill rack for about 10 minutes, turning frequently and brushing with any remaining marinade, until flecked with brown at the edges.

LEEK AND GOATS' CHEESE BURGERS

PREPARATION TIME 15 minutes, plus 4 hours chilling

COOKING TIME 20–25 minutes

SERVES 4

300g/10oz potatoes
75g/3oz soft goats' cheese
125g/4½oz leeks, finely chopped
1 tbsp unsalted butter
50g/2oz feta cheese, crumbled
25g/1oz/½ cup fresh breadcrumbs
sea salt and freshly ground black pepper
olive oil, for brushing
green salad and/or Mayonnaise
(see page 155), to serve

Peel and chop the potatoes into small chunks and boil for 10–15 minutes or until tender, then drain well. Return to the pan over a low heat and shake the pan gently to dry the potatoes. Remove from the heat. Mash the potatoes and beat in the goats' cheese.

Fry the leeks in the butter until very soft and dry. Beat them into the potato with the feta cheese, breadcrumbs and seasoning, using plenty of black pepper. Transfer to a plate, cover and chill for at least 4 hours.

With floured hands, shape into eight burgers about 6.5cm/2½in in diameter. Brush with oil. Cook on an oiled grill rack for about 3 minutes until browned and crisp, then turn over and cook on the other side. Serve with a green salad and/or mayonnaise.

HONEY-GLAZED SQUASH WEDGES WITH SESAME SEEDS

PREPARATION TIME 10 minutes

COOKING TIME 20–30 minutes

SERVES 4

1 large butternut squash, cut into wedges

6 tbsp clear honey

2 tbsp pumpkin seed oil

2 tbsp sesame seeds

sea salt and freshly ground black pepper

Place the squash wedges on a double layer of foil and drizzle over the honey and oil. Sprinkle over the sesame seeds and season generously. Fold over the sides of the foil and twist the edges together to seal tightly.

Cook the parcels on the edge of the grill rack for 20–30 minutes, turning them over a couple of times so that the squash cooks evenly.

SQUASH WEDGES WITH THYME AND GARLIC

PREPARATION TIME 10 minutes

COOKING TIME 15–18 minutes

SERVES 4

900g/2lb deseeded squash, cut into wedges

2 tbsp olive oil

2 plump garlic cloves, finely chopped

leaves from 2 sprigs of thyme

salt and freshly ground black pepper

Tomato Tartare Sauce (see page 156), to serve

Par-boil the squash wedges for 5 minutes. Drain, pat dry, and, while still warm, toss with the olive oil, garlic, thyme and seasoning.

Cook on an oiled grill rack for 5–6 minutes on each side until softened and charred. Serve with tomato tartare sauce.

ARTICHOKES WITH PARSLEY AND LEMON BUTTER

PREPARATION TIME 20 minutes, plus 1 hour marinating

COOKING TIME 25–30 minutes

SERVES 4

4 globe artichokes

lemon juice

5 tbsp olive oil

sea salt and freshly ground black pepper

PARSLEY AND LEMON BUTTER

1 garlic clove, peeled

50g/2oz/3½ tbsp unsalted butter

1 tbsp finely chopped flat-leaf parsley leaves

1–1½ tbsp lemon juice

Make the butter by blanching the garlic in simmering water for 5 minutes. Drain well, then mash to a paste. Beat the butter with a fork or wooden spoon until softened. Gradually work in the garlic paste, then the parsley, lemon juice and seasoning. Leave in a cool place for several hours for the flavours to infuse.

Snap off the artichoke stems near the base. Boil the artichokes in water acidulated with the juice of half a lemon for 10 minutes. Drain, leave until cool enough to handle, then trim off the outer layer of leaves.

Cut the artichokes into quarters and brush the cut surfaces with lemon juice. Scrape out the hairy choke and halve the quarters.

Lay the artichokes in a single layer in a shallow, non-metallic dish. Whisk together the olive oil, 2 tablespoons of lemon juice and seasoning. Pour over the artichokes, turn them over to make sure they are evenly coated, then cover and leave for an hour or so, or until needed.

Lift the artichokes from the dish and cook, straight-side down, on an oiled grill for 5–8 minutes until well patched with brown (don't worry if the leaves start to char). Turn the artichokes over and cook for a further 5–8 minutes until just tender.

Meanwhile, warm the butter gently on the side of the grill rack. Serve the artichokes immediately with the butter for dipping.

GRILLED LEEKS NIÇOISE

PREPARATION TIME 10 minutes

COOKING TIME 5 minutes

SERVES 2

200g/7oz baby leeks

150ml/5fl oz/⅔ cup extra virgin olive oil, plus extra for brushing

grated zest and juice of 1 lemon

sea salt and freshly ground black pepper

4 vine-ripened tomatoes, deseeded and chopped

1 tbsp capers

6 black olives, halved and pitted

2–4 salted anchovy fillets, rinsed, dried and chopped

handful of chopped parsley and basil leaves

Brush the leeks with oil and cook on an oiled grill rack for 5 minutes, turning once, until softened and marked with charred lines.

Meanwhile, whisk the oil with the lemon juice and seasoning until emulsified, or shake them together in a screw-topped jar.

Transfer the leeks to a plate, or plates, and pour over the dressing. Scatter over the remaining ingredients. Serve warm or at room temperature.

CHICORY WITH STILTON AND WALNUTS

PREPARATION TIME 10 minutes

COOKING TIME 7–12 minutes

SERVES 4

2 large or 4 small heads of chicory/endive, halved lengthways, cored

1 tbsp mild olive oil, plus extra for brushing

2 ripe but firm pears, thickly sliced

2 tbsp walnut oil

juice of 1 small lemon

1½ tsp thyme leaves

175g/6oz Stilton cheese, crumbled

50g/2oz/½ cup walnut halves, chopped

Brush the chicory/endive heads with olive oil and cook on an oiled grill rack, turning and brushing regularly, for 7–9 minutes for smaller heads, 10–12 minutes for larger ones, until softened and charred.

Meanwhile, cook the pear slices on the grill rack until softened.

Whisk the tablespoon of olive oil with the walnut oil and lemon juice.

Transfer the chicory/endive to warmed plates and season. Place the pears on top and immediately scatter over the cheese, then the thyme leaves. Trickle over the walnut oil mixture, sprinkle with the nuts and serve.

STUFFED ONIONS

PREPARATION TIME 15 minutes

COOKING TIME 20–25 minutes

SERVES 4

4 large onions, about 300g/10oz each, peeled

1 tbsp unsalted butter

1 large leek, chopped

leaves from 4 thyme sprigs

2 tbsp chopped parsley leaves

115g/4oz feta cheese, crumbled

8 sun-dried tomato halves in oil, drained and sliced

6 oil-cured black olives, pitted and chopped

2 egg yolks

freshly ground black pepper

Trim the root ends of the onions but do not cut them off completely because they hold the layers together. Cut each onion in half from top to bottom. Remove the inner layers of each onion half, leaving a shell two layers thick. Chop the removed layers.

Add the onion shells to a saucepan of boiling water, lower the heat and simmer for 10 minutes. Lift from the water with a slotted spoon and leave upside down to drain.

Meanwhile, melt the butter in a heavy-based frying pan. Add the chopped onion and cook over a very low heat until very soft and golden. Add the leek about three-quarters of the way through. Stir in the thyme and parsley, leave to cool slightly, then add the cheese, sun-dried tomatoes, olives and egg yolks. Season with plenty of black pepper.

Place each onion shell upright and pile the filling into the shells.

Cook the stuffed onions towards the side of the grill rack for 10–15 minutes until the shells are tender and the filling is warmed through.

VEGETABLE FAJITAS WITH AVOCADO AND TOMATO RELISH

PREPARATION TIME 10 minutes, plus 4 hours marinating

COOKING TIME 30 minutes

SERVES 6

2 red and 2 yellow peppers, deseeded and quartered

3 courgettes/zucchini, sliced diagonally

2 aubergines/eggplants, sliced diagonally

175g/6oz baby corn, halved lengthways

3 mild red chillies

6 tbsp olive oil

2 tbsp chopped mixed parsley, oregano and thyme leaves

juice of 1 lime

freshly ground black pepper

18 tortillas, 20cm/8in in diameter

sour cream, coriander/cilantro leaves and lime wedges, to serve

AVOCADO AND TOMATO RELISH

1 large avocado, pitted and finely chopped

3 tbsp lime juice

½ red chilli, deseeded and finely chopped

1 vine-ripened plum tomato, deseeded and diced

½ red onion, finely diced

handful of coriander/cilantro leaves, chopped

Put all the vegetables, including the chillies, into a large bowl. Mix together the olive oil, herbs, lime juice and black pepper. Stir into the vegetables, cover, then leave to marinate for about 4 hours, stirring occasionally.

Meanwhile, make the relish by tossing the ingredients together. Cover and chill for 30 minutes.

Lift the vegetables from the marinade and cook on an oiled grill rack until softened and lightly charred. Remove the vegetables that are cooked first as soon as they are ready, put into a bowl and cover with clingfilm/plastic wrap.

Meanwhile, warm the tortillas for 30 seconds on each side on the grill rack.

When the chillies are cool enough to handle, cut off the tops. Chop them, discarding the seeds.

Divide the vegetables and chillies among the tortillas. Top with avocado relish, spoon on some sour cream and fold over. Serve with coriander/cilantro and lime wedges.

FENNEL WEDGES WITH PARMESAN DRESSING

PREPARATION TIME 10 minutes

COOKING TIME 8–10 minutes

SERVES 4

4 small fennel bulbs

sea salt and freshly ground black pepper

olive oil for brushing

PARMESAN DRESSING

1 tbsp lemon juice

1 tbsp lemon zest

1 tbsp white wine vinegar

1 tsp Dijon mustard

120ml/4fl oz/½ cup extra virgin olive oil

2 tbsp freshly grated Parmesan cheese

Trim the fennel bulbs (reserve the feathery leaves), then cut into thick wedges. Brush with olive oil, thread onto oiled skewers and season.

Cook on an oiled grill rack for 8–10 minutes, turning occasionally, until the fennel is slightly soft and lightly charred. For softer fennel, cook for a little longer, further from the heat.

Meanwhile, make the dressing by whisking all the ingredients together. Season to taste.

Serve the fennel with the dressing poured over and sprinkled with the reserved feathery tops. (If the fennel bulbs don't have their feathery tops, substitute herb fennel.)

MINIATURE BOK CHOI WITH BALSAMIC DRESSING

PREPARATION TIME 5 minutes

COOKING TIME 8 minutes

SERVES 4

8 miniature bok choi

1 tbsp groundnut oil, plus extra for brushing

1 tbsp balsamic vinegar, plus extra for sprinkling

sea salt and freshly ground black pepper

Brush the bok choi with groundnut oil and sprinkle with balsamic vinegar. Cook on an oiled grill rack for about 4 minutes on each side until softened and marked with charred lines.

Meanwhile, make the dressing by combining the groundnut oil with the balsamic vinegar and seasoning.

Remove the bok choi from the grill rack and trickle over the dressing. Serve immediately.

SPINACH-FILLED TOMATOES WITH ROQUEFORT TOPPING

PREPARATION TIME 10 minutes

COOKING TIME 15 minutes

SERVES 4

4 large plum tomatoes, halved lengthways

2 tsp olive oil

1 shallot, finely chopped

1 garlic clove, finely chopped

175g/6oz frozen spinach, thawed and squeezed dry

50–75g/2–3oz Roquefort cheese, sliced

sea salt and freshly ground black pepper

Carefully scoop the pulp from the tomatoes. Sprinkle the inside of the shells with salt, turn them upside down and leave to drain. Chop the tomato flesh.

Heat the oil in a small frying pan, add the shallot and garlic and fry until softened, stirring occasionally. Add the chopped tomato flesh and heat, stirring, until the moisture has evaporated. Stir in the spinach, season and heat through.

Stand the tomatoes on a plate, cut-side up. Pack the spinach mixture into the tomato cups and top with a slice of cheese. Season with black pepper.

Cook the tomatoes on an oiled grill rack for about 4–6 minutes until the tomatoes are lightly charred and slightly softened. Do not allow them to become too soft otherwise they will be difficult to transfer to a serving plate.

GARLICKY POTATO SLICES

PREPARATION TIME 10 minutes

COOKING TIME 20–25 minutes

SERVES 4

550g/1¼lb unpeeled potatoes

2 garlic cloves

4 tbsp extra virgin olive oil

sea salt and freshly ground black pepper

handful of thyme or rosemary sprigs,
for cooking (optional)

Cook the potatoes in their skins in boiling water until just tender. Drain and, when cool enough to handle, cut into 1cm/½in thick slices. Season the potatoes with plenty of black pepper.

Crush the garlic with a pinch of salt, then mix with the oil. Brush over the potato slices.

Put the herb twigs on the fire, if using. Cook the potato slices on an oiled grill rack for 5 minutes on each side until the outsides are crisp and lightly charred, turning the slices halfway through.

SAUCES, SALSAS
& MARINADES

The recipes in this chapter can all be used to turn plain food into barbecued treats. Most marinades are mixtures of oil (which moistens the food), an acid ingredient (which tenderizes), and flavourings. Marinades are best made in advance (especially if the food will not be marinated for long) to allow the flavours to develop. Don't overdo the oil as this can cause a flare-up.

Leave foods to marinate or absorb a rub or paste in a cool place rather than the refrigerator, to avoid dulling the flavour. If foods are refrigerated, return them to room temperature 30–60 minutes before cooking. The more tender a food, the shorter the time it should be marinated, otherwise the acid in a marinade will make it soft. Use non-metallic dishes for marinating because acids do not react with them. Allow about 75–120ml/3–4fl oz/⅓–½ cup of marinade per 450g/ 1lb food. Cutting slashes in food will allow the marinade or rub to penetrate. Drain and pat dry marinated food before cooking (moisture prevents it browning), and scrape off any particles such as herbs.

Sugar-based mixtures give a sweet, rich coating to the food. However, they can burn, so are best brushed on the food halfway through cooking or just before the end. Herb and spice rubs, which give a deliciously crisp finish, can be either rubbed into the food or combined with a little oil first.

PESTO

PREPARATION TIME 10 minutes

SERVES 4

2 garlic cloves, chopped

2 handfuls of basil leaves

50g/2oz/heaped ⅓ cup pine nuts

150ml/5fl oz/heaped ⅓ cup olive oil

50g/2oz/⅔ cup Parmesan cheese, freshly grated

salt and freshly ground black pepper

Put the garlic, basil and pine nuts into a small blender or food processor. Mix to a paste. With the motor running, slowly pour in the oil to make a creamy paste.

Add the cheese, season to taste and mix briefly.

BASIL AND GRILLED TOMATO PESTO

PREPARATION TIME 10 minutes

COOKING TIME 5–10 minutes

SERVES 4–6

350g/12oz vine-ripened tomatoes

40g/1½oz basil leaves

2 garlic cloves, chopped

50g/2oz/½ cup blanched almonds, chopped

50g/2oz/½ cup walnut halves, chopped

120ml/4fl oz/½ cup fruity olive oil

50g/2oz pecorino cheese, freshly grated

salt and freshly ground black pepper

sun-dried tomato paste or a pinch of sugar (optional)

Preheat the grill and line the grill pan with foil. Grill the tomatoes, turning them frequently, until they are blistered and lightly charred. Leave until cool enough to handle, then remove the blackened patches.

Put the grilled tomatoes, basil leaves, garlic, nuts and a little of the oil into a small blender or food processor. Pulse until chopped together.

With the motor running, slowly pour in the oil to make a paste. Add the cheese. Season and add a little tomato paste or sugar, if necessary.

MAYONNAISE

PREPARATION TIME 10 minutes

SERVES 4–6

2 egg yolks, at room temperature

1 tsp Dijon mustard, or to taste

2–3 tsp white wine vinegar or lemon juice

salt and freshly ground black pepper

300ml/10fl oz/1¼ cups mild olive oil,
    at room temperature

Put the egg yolks, mustard, vinegar or lemon juice and a pinch of salt into a blender. Mix for about 10 seconds until blended, then, with the motor running, pour in the oil in a slow, steady stream until the mixture is thick and creamy.

Adjust the seasoning, levels of mustard and vinegar or lemon juice, if necessary. Store in a closed jar in the refrigerator for up to 3 days.

SUN-DRIED TOMATO AND GARLIC MAYONNAISE

PREPARATION TIME 10 minutes

SERVES 4

2 egg yolks

4 garlic cloves, crushed

juice of ½ lemon, or to taste

250ml/8fl oz olive oil

3½ tbsp oil from the sun-dried tomatoes

8 sun-dried tomato halves in oil, drained and
    finely chopped

salt and freshly ground black pepper

Put the egg yolks, garlic and lemon juice into a blender or food processor. Mix briefly. With the motor running, slowly pour in the oils until the mixture forms a thick cream.

Transfer to a bowl, stir in the chopped sun-dried tomatoes and season to taste, adding a little more lemon juice, if necessary.

AÏOLI

PREPARATION TIME 4 minutes

SERVES 4

6 plump garlic cloves, crushed
2 egg yolks, at room temperature
juice of 1 small lemon, plus extra, to taste
425ml/15 fl oz/1⅔ cups olive oil
3 tbsp wholegrain mustard
freshly ground black pepper

Put the garlic, egg yolks and lemon juice in a blender and mix. With the motor running, slowly pour in the olive oil until the mixture becomes the consistency of thick cream. Transfer to a bowl, stir in the mustard and season to taste.

RAITA

PREPARATION TIME 5 minutes

SERVES 4

½ cucumber, deseeded
1 small garlic clove, finely chopped
150ml/5fl oz/1⅔ cups Greek yogurt
2 tbsp chopped mint leaves
salt and freshly ground black pepper

Coarsely grate the cucumber and drain on kitchen paper. Combine the cucumber with the garlic, yogurt, mint and seasoning.

TOMATO TARTARE SAUCE

   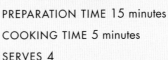

PREPARATION TIME 15 minutes

COOKING TIME 5 minutes

SERVES 4

3 tbsp white wine vinegar
½ shallot, finely chopped
4 black peppercorns, lightly crushed
a few tarragon stalks, coarsely chopped
120ml/4fl oz/½ cup Mayonnaise
   (see page 154)
1 tsp Dijon mustard
2 plum tomatoes, deseeded and finely chopped
2 tbsp finely chopped pitted green olives
2 tbsp gherkins, finely chopped

Boil the vinegar in a small saucepan with the shallot, peppercorns and tarragon until the liquid has reduced to 1 teaspoon. Leave to cool.

Mix the mayonnaise and mustard together and strain the vinegar into the mustard mayonnaise. Stir in the remaining ingredients. Taste for seasoning.

HOME-MADE TOMATO KETCHUP

PREPARATION TIME 10 minutes

COOKING TIME 20–30 minutes

MAKES 700ml/24fl oz/3 cups

1.5kg/3lb tomatoes, chopped

1 fleshy red pepper, deseeded and sliced

2 red onions, chopped

½ tsp paprika

175ml/6fl oz spiced red wine vinegar*

Put the tomatoes, red pepper, red onion and paprika into a saucepan with the vinegar. Simmer until thick, stirring occasionally.

Press through a nylon or plastic sieve, return the juice to the rinsed pan and boil vigorously until thick. Pour into warmed, very clean jars, cover and leave to cool. Store in the refrigerator or other cold, dark place for up to 3 months.

* To make the spiced red wine vinegar, bring 1 teaspoon celery seeds, 1 small mace blade and 1 teaspoon black peppercorns to the boil in the vinegar, then cover and leave to marinate for a day before straining and using.

ROASTED TOMATO SALSA

PREPARATION TIME 10 minutes

COOKING TIME 6–7

SERVES 4–6

6 ripe tomatoes, halved

2–3 tbsp lime juice

2 tbsp olive oil

3 tbsp chopped coriander/cilantro leaves

5 spring onions/scallions, finely chopped

2 garlic cloves, finely chopped

1 small red chilli, deseeded and chopped

1 tsp ground cumin

salt

Put the tomatoes, skin-side down, on an oiled grill rack and cook for about 6–7 minutes until slightly softened and the skin is charred in patches.

Remove from the grill rack, leave until cool enough to handle, then peel off the skins. Coarsely chop the flesh and mix with the remaining ingredients. Serve warm.

PINEAPPLE AND MACADAMIA NUT SALSA

PREPARATION TIME 15 minutes

SERVES 4

1 small pineapple

25g/1oz/¼ cup macadamia nuts, chopped

1 red onion, finely chopped

1 garlic clove, finely chopped

1 tbsp light soy sauce

3 tbsp lime juice

freshly ground black pepper

Using a large, sharp knife, cut the top and bottom from the pineapple. Stand the pineapple on a board and, cut off the peel. Make sure all the 'eyes' are removed. Cut the pineapple into quarters from top to bottom, then cut out the core. Chop the flesh finely and put into a bowl.

Add all the remaining ingredients to the bowl and toss together.

AVOCADO, TOMATO AND RED PEPPER SALSA

PREPARATION TIME 10 minutes,
      plus 30 minutes chilling

COOKING TIME 20 minutes

SERVES 4

1 red pepper

2 large, ripe avocados

1 garlic clove, finely chopped

1 plum tomato, finely chopped

1 small red onion, very finely chopped

1 red chilli, deseeded and finely chopped

juice of 1 small lime

4 tbsp chopped coriander/cilantro leaves

salt and freshly ground black pepper

Cook the red pepper on an oiled grill rack on a barbecue, or under a preheated hot grill, turning occasionally, until well charred and soft. Leave until cool enough to handle, then remove the skin and discard the seeds. Chop the flesh very finely. Put into a bowl.

Peel the avocados, remove the stones and chop the flesh finely. Add to the bowl with the remaining ingredients. Toss gently to combine. Cover and chill for 30 minutes.

RED PEPPER, BLACK OLIVE AND CAPER RELISH

PREPARATION TIME 10 minutes

COOKING TIME 10 minutes

SERVES 4

3 red peppers

150g/5oz pitted oil-cured kalamata olives, chopped

60g/2½oz capers (in balsamic vinegar), coarsely chopped

2½ tbsp coarsely chopped basil leaves

2½ tbsp coarsely chopped flat-leaf parsley leaves

2 tbsp olive oil

salt and freshly ground black pepper

Preheat the grill. Grill the peppers, turning frequently, until the skins char and blister. Leave until cool enough to handle, then peel off and discard the skins, seeds and core. Chop the flesh.

Mix the pepper flesh with the olives, capers, herbs and oil. Season to taste, then cover and chill until required.

JAMAICAN JERK SEASONING

PREPARATION TIME 5 minutes

SERVES 4

5 red chillies, deseeded and chopped

2 spring onions/scallions, chopped

1 tbsp dried thyme

1 tbsp dried basil

2 tbsp orange juice

2 tbsp white wine vinegar

1 tbsp yellow mustard seeds

1 tsp ground allspice

1 tsp ground cloves

salt and freshly ground black pepper

Put all the ingredients into a blender and mix to a thick sauce. If necessary, add a little more orange juice or vinegar to obtain the right consistency.

DESSERTS

Barbecued desserts are the most appropriate and delicious way to end your meal. Some people might be surprised at the variety of desserts that can be cooked on a grill rack and if the grill rack is covered, the range is even greater.

Choose fruits that are ripe but not too soft, and remove them from the grill rack before they overcook. Tropical fruits such as pineapple and mango are always popular, but there are many others that work equally well: pears, peaches, bananas cooked in their skins – all become wonderful treats when served sizzling and lightly caramelized from a grill rack. Add some spices, either simply sprinkled on or in a marinade, baste or butter, and they become exotic.

Individual fruits or combinations can be enclosed in foil parcels and cooked on the grill rack. This is particularly good for fragile items such as strawberries and raspberries and for fruits that are too ripe and soft to be cooked directly on the grill rack. Slices of sweet breads and cakes also grill well, and provide bases for the fruit, making more substantial desserts.

Clean any particles of savoury food off the grill rack before cooking desserts on it. If possible, cook the fruit on an oiled fine mesh grill rack or in an oiled hinged grill basket, for ease of turning and lifting.

STUFFED PEACHES

PREPARATION TIME 10 minutes

COOKING TIME 8–10 minutes

SERVES 4

25g/1oz amaretti biscuits, fairly finely crushed

50g/2oz Madeira/yellow sponge cake, crumbed

4 tbsp amaretto liqueur

4 ripe but firm large peaches, halved and pitted

8 tbsp orange juice

25g/1oz/¼ cup flaked/slivered almonds, toasted

Mix together the amaretti biscuits, cake crumbs and 2 tablespoons of amaretto. Divide among the hollows in the peaches.

Combine the remaining amaretto with the orange juice.

Put two peach halves on a piece of foil that is large enough to enclose them. Fold up the sides of the foil. Sprinkle one quarter of the nuts over the filling. Pour one quarter of the orange juice mixture over. Fold the foil loosely over the peaches and pleat the sides together to make a secure parcel. Repeat with the remaining peach halves.

Cook on a grill rack for 8–10 minutes until the peaches have softened and warmed through.

CARAMELIZED APPLES WITH BRIOCHE TOASTS

PREPARATION TIME 10 minutes

COOKING TIME 4–5 minutes

SERVES 4

4 dessert apples, cored and thickly sliced

juice of 1 lime

2 tbsp caster/granulated sugar

1 tsp ground cinnamon

4 tbsp unsalted butter, melted

4 thick slices brioche

Greek yogurt, to serve

Sprinkle the cut surfaces of apple with lime juice.

Stir the sugar and cinnamon together, then stir half of the mixture into the warm butter until the sugar has dissolved. Brush over the brioche and apple slices.

Cook the apples on an oiled grill rack for 4–5 minutes, turning once, until browned. Add the brioche slices to the side of the grill rack a couple of minutes later and keep an eye on them as they can burn easily.

Remove the brioche slices to plates. Cut the apples into halves or quarters and put onto the brioche slices. Sprinkle with the remaining sugar and cinnamon. Serve with Greek yogurt.

CHOCOLATE BRIOCHE SANDWICHES

PREPARATION TIME 10 minutes

COOKING TIME 5 minutes

SERVES 4

8 slices brioche

good-quality apricot conserve, for spreading

150–175g/5–6oz good-quality plain/bittersweet chocolate, grated

vanilla ice cream, to serve

Spread one side of each brioche slice with conserve. Divide the chocolate among half the apricot-covered slices and cover with the other slices, apricot-side down. Press each sandwich together.

Cook on an oiled grill rack until the underside is beginning to colour. Turn carefully and repeat on the other side until the chocolate has melted; press gently with a fish slice two or three times.

Serve straight away, either on their own or accompanied by vanilla ice cream.

PAPAYA WITH CHILLI LIME SYRUP

PREPARATION TIME 5 minutes

COOKING TIME 10 minutes

SERVES 4

8 tbsp light soft brown sugar

1 red chilli, deseeded and cut into thin strips

zest of 2 limes, cut into fine strips

juice of 2 limes

2 papayas

Make the syrup by putting the sugar, chilli and 200ml/7fl oz/generous ¾ cup of water in a saucepan and bringing to the boil. Reduce the heat and simmer for 5 minutes to make a syrup. Add the lime zest and juice and pour into a jug.

Cut the papayas into thin wedges, brush with some of the syrup and cook on an oiled grill rack for about 4 minutes until lightly caramelized. Serve with the remaining syrup.

FRUIT KEBABS WITH HONEY, ORANGE AND PECAN SAUCE

PREPARATION TIME 10 minutes

COOKING TIME 6–8 minutes

SERVES 4

2 apples, cored and cut into wedges

2 pears, cored and cut into wedges

6 plums, pitted and cut into wedges

single/light cream, to serve

HONEY, ORANGE AND PECAN SAUCE

1 orange

2 tbsp clear honey

50g/2oz/3½ tbsp unsalted butter

1 tbsp icing/confectioners' sugar

5cm/2in rosemary sprig

50g/2oz/½ cup shelled pecans

Make the sauce by paring the zest from the orange and cutting it into fine shreds. Blanch the shreds in boiling water for 1 minute. Drain and repeat once more. Set aside.

Squeeze the juice from the orange and pour into a small saucepan with the honey, butter and icing/confectioners' sugar. Add the rosemary and heat gently for 5 minutes, stirring until evenly mixed.

Thread the fruits alternately onto skewers. Brush the fruit with the honey mixture and cook on an oiled grill rack until sizzling and lightly browned.

Meanwhile, discard the rosemary from the sauce, add the pecans and reheat.

Transfer the kebabs to plates, pour some of the sauce around them and sprinkle over the blanched orange zest shreds. Serve with cream.

PEARS WITH CHOCOLATE SAUCE

PREPARATION TIME 5 minutes

COOKING TIME 12–15 minutes

SERVES 4

4 ripe but firm pears

CHOCOLATE SAUCE

75g/3oz good-quality plain/bittersweet chocolate (at least 70% cocoa solids), chopped

50g/2oz/½ cup cocoa powder

25g/1oz/2 tbsp caster/granulated sugar, or to taste

150ml/5fl oz/⅔ cup boiling water

Make the sauce by melting the chocolate in 120ml/4fl oz/½ cup of the boiling water in a small bowl placed over a saucepan of hot water. Stir regularly until smooth.

Dissolve the cocoa powder and sugar in the remaining boiling water, then pour into the melted chocolate, stirring, until smooth. Set aside.

Cut the pears into quarters lengthways and remove the cores. Cook on an oiled grill rack (in an oiled hinged grilling basket for ease of turning) for about 4 minutes on each side until warmed, slightly softened and lightly charred.

Meanwhile, warm the bowl of sauce over a saucepan of hot water on the side of the grill rack. Serve the pears with the warm sauce poured over.

FIGS WITH GOATS' CHEESE, HONEY AND THYME

PREPARATION TIME 10 minutes

COOKING TIME 5–6 minutes

SERVES 4

12 ripe but not too soft figs, halved lengthways
8 tbsp soft mild goats' cheese
thyme leaves, for sprinkling
4 tbsp clear honey

Spread each fig half with goats' cheese.
Sprinkle lightly with thyme and trickle over
the honey.

Cook the figs on an oiled grill rack over low
heat for about 5–6 minutes until soft.

FUDGY BANANAS WITH RUM

PREPARATION TIME 5 minutes

COOKING TIME 4–5 minutes

SERVES 4

4 bananas, peeled
a knob of unsalted butter
75g/3oz vanilla fudge, coarsely chopped
4 tbsp rum
vanilla ice cream, to serve

Cut a slit along the length of each banana,
but don't cut right through.

Place each banana on a large square of
buttered foil and fill the slits with fudge.
Fold up the edges of the foil and pour the
rum over the bananas. Twist the edges of
the foil together to seal.

Grill for 4–5 minutes until heated through.
Serve with vanilla ice cream.

CARAMEL ORANGES

PREPARATION TIME 15 minutes

COOKING TIME 12–14 minutes

SERVES 4

4 large oranges

melted unsalted butter, for brushing

1–2 tbsp brown sugar

2 tbsp Orange Nassau, Cointreau, Grand Marnier or other orange liqueur

vanilla ice cream, to serve

Working over a bowl to catch any juice, carefully cut away all the orange skin and white pith. Reserve some of the skin. Cut across each orange to make six slices.

Remove the pith from the peel, then cut the peel into very fine shreds. Blanch these in boiling water for 2–3 minutes. Drain and dry.

Cut four double-thickness squares of foil that are large enough to wrap loosely around an orange. Butter the middle of each square thoroughly with unsalted butter.

Divide the slices among the pieces of well-buttered foil. Fold up the sides of the foil. Divide the orange juice from the bowl, the sugar and liqueur among the oranges, then twist the edges of the foil firmly together to make roomy but tightly sealed parcels.

Cook the parcels of oranges on the side of the barbecue for about 10 minutes.

Carefully transfer the cooked parcels to serving plates and open up the foil. Add a scoop of vanilla ice cream.

SUMMER BERRY PARCELS
WITH CARDAMOM CREAM

PREPARATION TIME 15 minutes, plus 30 minutes infusion

COOKING TIME 4–5 minutes

SERVES 4

450g/1lb prepared mixed red summer fruits, such as ripe but firm strawberries (halved if large), pitted

cherries, raspberries, blackberries and blueberries

4 tbsp raspberry eau-de-vie, white rum or peach schnapps

3–4 tbsp golden caster/granulated sugar

5 tbsp orange juice

1 tbsp lemon juice

CARDAMOM CREAM

2–3 cardamom pods, split

about 1½ tsp caster/granulated sugar, or to taste

300ml/10fl oz/1¼ cups single/light or whipping cream

Make the cream by heating the cardamom and sugar in the cream until it boils. Remove from the heat, cover the pan and leave to infuse for 30 minutes. Strain, cool completely and then chill.

Divide the fruits among four squares of heavy-duty foil large enough to enclose the fruits.

Warm the eau-de-vie, caster/granulated sugar and fruit juices in a small saucepan until the sugar has dissolved. Pour the syrup over the fruits.

Fold the foil loosely over the fruits and twist the edges together firmly to secure. Put the parcels on the side of a grill rack and cook for 4–5 minutes until heated through.

Taste the cardamom cream for sweetness and serve with the fruit parcels.

PINEAPPLE, MANGO, PEAR AND APRICOT KEBABS WITH MAPLE YOGURT SAUCE

PREPARATION TIME 15 minutes

COOKING TIME 5 minutes

SERVES 4

1 small pineapple, peeled

1 mango, peeled, pitted and cut into 2.5cm/ 1in chunks

1 large ripe but firm pear, cored and cut into 2.5cm/1in chunks

4 ripe but firm apricots, pitted and quartered

2 tbsp maple syrup

1 tbsp brandy or lemon juice

MAPLE YOGURT SAUCE

3–4 tbsp maple syrup

1 tbsp brandy

150ml/5fl oz/⅔ cup yogurt

Make the maple yogurt sauce by stirring the maple syrup and brandy into the yogurt. Cover and chill until required.

Quarter the pineapple lengthways, cut away the core, then cut the flesh into 2.5cm/1in chunks.

Thread all the fruits alternately onto soaked wooden skewers.

Combine the maple syrup with the brandy or lemon juice and brush over the fruits. Cook on an oiled grill rack for 5 minutes until piping hot and flecked with gold, turning regularly.

Serve the kebabs with some of the maple yogurt sauce trickled over. Serve the remaining sauce separately.

INDEX